MW01277743

WHERE IS HERE?
THE DRAMA OF IMMIGRATION
Volume I

WHERE IS HERE?

THE DRAMA OF IMMIGRATION
Volume I

EDITED BY Damiano Pietropaolo

Where Is Here? The Drama of Immigration (Vol. I)
first published 2005 by
Scirocco Drama
An imprint of J. Gordon Shillingford Publishing Inc.
© 2005 the Authors

Editor: Damiano Pietropaolo
Scirocco Drama Editor: Glenda MacFarlane
Cover design by Doowah Design Inc.
Cover photo courtesy of Library and Archives Canada
Printed and bound in Canada

We acknowledge the financial support of the Manitoba Arts Council, The Canada
Council for the Arts and the Government of Canada through the Book Publishing
Industry Development Program (BPIDP) for our publishing program.

*This is for Dave Carley, whose collaboration over the years
has gone a long way to ensure an ever-renewing voice for
Canadian Radio Drama.*

Canadian Cataloguing in Publication Data

    Where is here?/a CBC radio drama anthology/Damiano
Pietropaolo, editor.

ISBN 0-920486-73-8 (v. 1). — ISBN 0-920486-87-8 (v. 2)

    1. Immigrants—Canada—Drama. 2. Canadian drama (English)—21st
century. I. Pietropaolo, Damiano

PS8309.I49W49 2005   C812'.608   C2005-900165-8

J. Gordon Shillingford Publishing
P.O. Box 86, RPO Corydon Avenue, Winnipeg, MB Canada R3M 3S3

Table of Contents

Preface

It is widely believed that Canada's destiny, culturally and historically, finds its fulfillment in being a nation, and that nationality is essential to identity. It seems to me, on the other hand, quite clear that we are moving towards a post-national world and that Canada has moved further in that direction than any of the smaller nations. What is important about the last century, in this country, is not that we have been a nation for a hundred years but that we have had a hundred years to make the transition from a pre-national to a post-national consciousness.

Northrop Frye, *The Modern Century*, 1967

For over thirty years, following a routine as monotonous and comforting as the rhythm of the old Red Rocket making its rambling way along College Street on its loop to High Park, I went for a haircut to Pino's Barber Shop on the corner of College and Clinton streets, in Toronto's Little Italy. The clientele consisted mainly of Old World peasants who arrived here during the last great wave of emigration from their now depopulated villages in Southern Italy. They dropped in daily for a chat, and only rarely for a haircut. Mostly they came for an old-fashioned shave, luxuriating in the knowledge that some things never change. Their stories pulled me to the little barbershop with the force of gravity. Caught in the deadly grip of nostalgia, they chattered away in their ancient dialect and listened to the radio blaring the soccer scores from Italy, their concentration broken only by the rumble of the Red Rocket. These old streetcars no longer ride the rails in Toronto, except as museum pieces. They can now be found on the streets of Cairo.

In 21st century Toronto, the most multicultural city in the world, the barbershop is no more. It was gobbled up by our hunger for post-national urbanism in what is now one of the trendiest neighbourhoods on the continent. Although spruced up, the shabby old red building still stands where, for generations, it bore witness to the ebb and flow of change that has taken Toronto from a pre-national to a post-national consciousness.

Some of the regulars had arrived in Canada on the *Queen Frederica*, the same ship on which my father, chasing after a dream of a rosier future for his four children, brought me here kicking and screaming; here, to this, the land of plenty across the wide open sea. On the deck of the *Queen Frederica*, I stood alongside the other children, all of us in our Sunday best and with fear in our hearts, struggling to hang on to the threads of our fathers' vision. Many of us improvised a temporary Old World piazza on the floating village of the ship's deck in the full knowledge that whatever friendships we forged would be as short-lived, and as unforgettable, as the *Queen Frederica*'s journey from Piraeus, to Naples, Genoa, Gibraltar on to Halifax and New York. Later we would come to realize that the journey into the New World is never-ending. Here, on board this floating Tower of Babel as we slowly approached Halifax harbour in the thickening fog, overcome with foreboding, and not speaking each other's language, we held hands in silence as Pier 21 readied to welcome us.

Toronto's College Street has been a destination for wave upon wave of newly arrived immigrants, and the barbershop was there, a home away from home, waiting. The barbershop itself was sandwiched between what was Cohen's fish market and a Greek Orthodox Church, just around the corner from the Jewish Health Bread Bakery and across the street from Winestock tailors. The local cinema comforted many an immigrant worker through a lonely Saturday night by radiating the solace of nostalgia from its large screen in Italian, Portuguese, and Spanish. Later it became the Golden Princess and catered to the latest arrivals, Chinese-speaking students from Hong Kong fleeing an even Older World for the promise of the New. It is now a repertory art film house and home to the annual international documentary festival Hot Docs.

The idea of a series of plays on the theme of immigration owes its origin to the richness of the stories heard in that barbershop which still haunts the corner of College and Clinton streets in Toronto. When we decided to commission a series of plays on the theme of immigration, the programming team for Sunday Showcase, the weekly radio drama program heard nationally on CBC Radio, felt that the best approach was to put out a proposal call [see appendix]. The call resulted in over 70 proposals from all corners of the country. It was an embarrassment of riches, both in terms of the great variety of stories on the immigrant experience, and the quality of the writing. The transition from a pre-national to a post-national consciousness described by Northrop Frye just as Canada was celebrating its 100th birthday as a nation, had certainly taken place. The evidence was in front of us, in all these proposals submitted by Canadian writers whose cultural horizons extend way beyond any notion of national boundaries.

The commissioning team, which included series script editor Dave Carley, contributing producer Kathleen Flaherty, Associate Producer M. Rosie Fernandez, and me, soon realized that to choose only three plays from such a wealth of good proposals was simply not enough. And so the original series of three plays evolved into the plays collected in these two volumes: *Where Is Here?* is an anthology of twelve original radio plays exploring our post-national consciousness.

In making our final selection we were guided above all by the power of the stories themselves and by the imaginative use of the medium of radio to tap into what playwright David Mamet, in his 1986 essay collection, *Writing in Restaurants*, believes to be our primal need for participatory narrative—for the story around the campfire—or in the barbershop. "More than any other dramatic medium," Mamet reminds us, "[radio] teaches the writer to concentrate on the essentials, because it throws into immediate relief that to characterize the people or the scene is to take time from the story—to weaken the story." When the final selection of the plays had been made, the primacy of a very specific narrative emerged: a tale of human beings migrating from all corners of the earth, stretching over continents and generations and gathering the vast diversity of stories that have made Canada the post-national country envisioned by Northrop Frye in 1967.

As in Donna Caruso's *Clothesline,* the narratives in these plays stretch all the way from Saskatchewan to Southern Italy, from Montreal to Cairo, from Toronto to Hong Kong and the Philippines, from Vancouver to the Punjab region of India. Although the plays themselves are in various formats, and feature a wide range of tones, from tragedy to broad comedy, they are united by a primal need to gather diverse experiences into common narrative. From the documentary approach of John Ng's *Joy Geen* and Sugith

Varughese's *Entry Denied*, to the lyrical memoir of Rishma Dunlop's *The Raj Kumari's Lullaby*. The journey back to the homeland of Marcia Johnson's *Say Ginger Ale* and Marco Micone's *Wanderers*, is in contrast with the speculative imagination of parallel universes in Ehab Lotayef's *Crossing Gibraltar*. The poignancy of a modern inter-cultural and interracial romance in Guillaume Vigneault's *Couscous* complements the hilarious misunderstandings that can occur when cultures clash, as in Marjorie Chan's *Spring Arrival*, or the dilemma faced by modern Canadian women whose roots still pull them back to a time they thought they had left behind, as in Marie-Beath Badian's *Novena* or Marty Chan's *The Gift*. The narratives in these plays link an Old World to an uncharted New World full of promises as vast as the Canadian geography itself. Memory of another time and place haunts the immigrant writer like a phantom limb.

Northrop Frye has also written that the problem facing Canadian writers in our post-national country is not "Who am I?" but "Where is here?" For the immigrant writer, this may not be a geographical question, but a temporal one, for "here" is more often than not in the past: "there," in the place left behind. In our post-national urban centers, such as Toronto, where 43% of the population is foreign-born, or Vancouver (37.5%), or Montreal (18.4%), Northrop Frye's question remains more relevant than ever. It's a question to which immigrants bring an existential, carnal understanding, as we embrace a dichotomized, disembodied sense of self: a post-national consciousness that straddles geography and time on its never-ending journey into the New World. In Micone's *Wanderers*, we find the young protagonist Nino, a native of Montreal, strolling the empty cobbled streets with his Italian-born father in an abandoned village in Southern Italy. There, in the stillness of a summer night they come to a stone dwelling without doors or windows. When Nino asks his father Luigi, "Where is home, Papa?" he replies that it is just around the corner by the gurgling stream. But the stream has dried up and only Luigi can hear its sound, locked away in his memory of the enchanted childhood in the village before it was depopulated by emigration. For poet Rishma Dunlop, the answer to Nino's question lies in a pilgrimage into language itself, where home can only be a "cradle made of words."

As for me and my house…the New World first appeared to me from the deck of the *Queen Frederica* as it docked at Pier 21 in the late

March sunshine of 1959. From there through the magical snow
shrouded landscapes of Nova Scotia, New Brunswick, Quebec and
Ontario glimmering in the winter sun, the long train ride took us to
Union Station and the barbershop in Little Italy. In this corner of
post-national Toronto, like on the deck of the *Queen Frederica*, the
New World and the Old float on the vast sea of memory that links
them, and the barbershop, a stubborn apparition from the Old, still
haunts the New like an obsession. The *Queen Frederica* and her sister
ships, the *Olympia*, the *Raffaello*, the *Vulturnia*, stopped unloading
their cargo of human souls long ago. Pier 21 now houses Canada's
Immigration Museum, but from 1928 to 1971 it was the gateway
through which over three million people first set foot on the land we
call Canada. Arthur J. Vaughn was one of many immigration
officers welcoming new arrivals into the country. In the memoir of
his experiences that concludes these two volumes we meet some of
the characters that people this series, immigrants leaving a past
behind for a future in a place that for many remains an
unanswerable question: "Where is here?" As I produced this series
of plays for broadcast, I often thought that on that sunny morning in
late March 1959, Mr. Vaughn and I met across a threshold that was
to permanently change, for both of us, our sense of who we are.

Damiano Pietropaolo
Executive Producer, "Where is Here"
CBC Radio January 23–February 27, 2005

The Raj Kumari's Lullaby

Rishma Dunlop

Rishma Dunlop

Rishma Dunlop was born in India and grew up in Beaconsfield, Quebec. Her recent books are *The Body of My Garden* (Mansfield Press, 2002), *Reading Like a Girl* (Black Moss Press, 2004), *Red Silk: An Anthology of South Asian Canadian Women Poets* (co-edited with Priscila Uppal, Mansfield Press, 2004), and the forthcoming *Naramata Road* (Mansfield Press, 2005). She was a finalist for the CBC Canada Council Award for Poetry in 1998 and a recipient of the Emily Dickinson Award in 2003. She is a professor of Literary Studies in the Faculty of Education and School of Women's Studies at York University in Toronto.

About the Play

Begins on May 28, 1990, in Beaconsfield, Quebec, the day of the narrator's father's funeral. The time frame of the play moves back into memory of the narrator's parents' lives in colonial and postcolonial India, the narrator's birth in 1956 and infancy in India. The narration then spans the period of time between 1958 travelling and immigrating to Ottawa, then moving to Beaconsfield on the West Island of Montreal in the early 1960's. The narration begins at the funeral home and continuously returns to it during the scenes as the narration moves in and out of memory and time.

Characters

NARRATOR: Adult woman in her forties, Canadian of East Indian descent, no accent. Her voice must reflect North American upbringing and a Canadian way of speaking, cultured, educated, eloquent, articulate voice, ability to imbue narration with poetic quality and to perform the poetry within the play in a seamless way as part of narration.

FATHER: Adult male of Punjabi, East Indian descent, educated under British rule. He does not speak with a heavy accent, cultured expression yet not the British accent of those educated in England. Scientist, capable of giving academic lectures. Kindness and loving nature reflected in voice particularly in exchanges with daughter and wife.

MOTHER: Adult woman of Punjabi, East Indian descent. Must not have heavy accent, educated under British rule in India. University educated and professional.

CANADIAN
VOICE: Adult male, business-like, reading letter from National Research Council in Ottawa.

VOICES: Gathering in funeral home. Soft greetings, expressions of sympathy as background noise. These move in and out of several scenes from beginning to end.

TEENAGE
VOICES: Party scene, 16–17 year olds at party.

ITALIAN VOICES:	Priests and nuns in Rome, blessing narrator as a little child travelling to Canada.
NARRATOR AS CHILD:	Small girl's voice, laughing with mother in snapshot scenes.
LITTLE BOY IN MONTREAL:	Around 5-6 years old.
GIRL GUIDES:	Voices at an actual meeting or staged, reciting Guide promise and law, as well as singing Taps (soldier's bugle call-song to close meeting) in unison. (Should be the sort of unruly chorus that happens with a group of pre-adolescent girls, some singing loudly off-key).
MISS DAMROL:	Ballet teacher. Woman in her thirties, British, clipped, formal, frosty, commanding presence.
INDIAN RELATIVES, GROUP OF WOMEN, AUNTIES:	Speaking Punjabi and English-mixed enough to convey meaning of Punjabi phrases in Section 13 (2).
REVEREND:	For beginnings of United Church wedding service in Section 16.

Cast

NARRATOR: .... Rahnuma Panthaky

FATHER: .... Ishwar Mooljee

MOTHER: .... Malika Mendez

OTHER VOICES: .... Barbara Worthy,
Vince Carlin, Quinn Roy

Production Credits

Producer/Director:............. Damiano Pietropaolo

Associate Producer: .... Rosie Fernandez

Original Music: .... Suba Sankaran

Script Editor: .... Dave Carley

Casting: .... Linda Grearson

Recording Engineer: .... Wayne Richards

Sound Effects: .... Anton Szabo

Prelude

Theme: based on Punjabi Lullaby "Soja Raj Kumari Soja." Original version by Kundan Lal Saigal, score by Panjak Mullick, originally in 1940 Bollywood film "Zindagi." Establish then fade to background and hold...

FATHER's
VOICE: *(Singing.) Soja Rajkumari soja*
Soja meethe sapne aayen
Soja pyari Rajkumari

Memory

NARRATOR: My childhood lullaby, the one my father sang to me each night at bedtime, stroking my hair back from my forehead. The Hindi and Punjabi words, my childhood tongues, lost languages to me now.
Soja RajKumari soja. Sleep little princess sleep.
Soja meethe sapne aayen. Sleep with sweet dreams.
Soja pyari RajKumari. Sleep beloved little princess.

FATHER's
VOICE: *(Reverb.)* Soja *beta*, sleep little one. Sleep child.

Voices, hushed greetings of people attending funeral, comforting family.

NARRATOR: It's all I can think about today, this lullaby, the childhood words, as I have returned home and we are gathered at the funeral home. My sisters and I have shed our western clothes and are dressed in the brilliant silk saris my father would have loved. Mine is blue like the lake near our childhood home, the blue of Lake St. Louis in Beaconsfield on the West Island of Montreal.

Fades to silence before the following.

NARRATOR: But my story begins many years ago in India.

Chirping, songs of birds, soft sound of water fountains splashing, sensibility of lush gardenscape...city sounds in distance.

I am born on October 19, 1956 in a nursing home in Poona, India, a city close to what is now called Mumbai, then called Bombay.

NURSE: *(Reverb.)* Jehangir Nursing Home, 32, Sassoon Road, Poona. Certificate No. 902. Date: 20th of October, 1956. Certified that In the above Nursing Home, Mrs. Narender Kartar Singh Delivered a Living Female Child on the 19th of October, 1956 at 2 AM. Sex: Female. Signed by the Assistant Lady Doctor.

Voices of mother and infant.

NARRATOR: In Poona, my mother tends to her infant daughter...her maidservant brings her tea and fresh flowers for her hair every morning.

Woman-servant's voice in Punjabi—serving tea, sound of tea being served, china cups, pouring from teapot.

My mother is a teacher, the daughter of a landowner, a farmer. She is a young woman who fought against tradition to get a higher education after convent school in Sialkote, Lahore, a school taught by British nuns. She went to Lady McLaughlin High School where half the teachers were British and the principal was Miss White. She was in Grade 9 when the partition happened and her family escaped the violence across the Pakistan border in the middle of the night. She got her B.A. at Government College Ludhiana and then she

convinced her father to let her go on to Teachers
College in Simla. She married my father only after
several years of a career of her own as an elementary
school teacher. My father was the son of a Supreme
Court judge, university educated with a Ph.D. in
biochemistry. My father courted my mother,
coming to the school to take photos of his nephew
who was in her class. This began several years of
love letters and family negotiations to arrange the
marriage.

Music: "Ancestors."

NARRATOR'S
POETIC VOICE: *(Reverb.)* I can hear my ancestors behind me in
another continent across the Indian Ocean crossing
the floors, soft sweep of sandals in my mother's
country. I was born there four decades ago at 2 AM.
My birth certificate reads *Living Female Child.* Today
my passport reads Nationality Canadian.[1] On the
back of my birth certificate is the red stamp from
the Department of National Health and Welfare,
registered October 1, 1959.

> *Indian bazaar, noise of bazaar, voices of street
> vendors, beggars, rick-shaws and drivers, fades as
> narration resumes.*

My mother's land is still there: scooters and
rickshaws navigating through crowded streets
full of billboards for Bollywood films,
dreamscapes of floating lotus ponds,
lush public gardens, the smells of decay and sweet
     jasmine,
bustling bazaars and stinking alleyways,
cities like Victorian London among palm trees and
     banyans,
the rivers marking the routes of cranes and egrets.
The ancestors are still there, with the last remnants
of the British Raj drinking chai scented with
cardamom, old women in desert white saris,
turbanned sirdars, the young women with amber

skin, hair and brows as black as crows' wings,
eyes of lionesses in heat, dressed in silks of
delirious hues, violent pinks, bangles and anklets
clinking they wander through foreign rooms in the
last daylight of the century painting their eyes
brush of sandalwood across the collarbone.
Somewhere out of them, alive or dead I have
sprung. Yet no one seems to recognize me.

> *"Ancestors"* —*out.*

No one.[2]

Coming to Canada

CANADIAN
VOICE: *Canadian male voice reading letter, fades under and then
                     resumes again.*

Office of the National Research Council
Ottawa, Canada
1958

Dear Dr. Singh:

We are pleased to inform you that you have been
selected as a recipient of a Postdoctoral Fellowship
with the National Research Council in Ottawa,
Canada. Our selection committee was impressed
with the calibre of your biochemical research and
publications on antibiotics and would like to invite
you to join its research team in pharmaceutical
research. The National Research Council is
currently recruiting international scientists to
enrich our research community. We would be
pleased to offer you a stipend and accommodation
for you and your family for a 24-month posting at
our headquarters in Ottawa.

We look forward to hearing from you and hope that
you will accept our offer. Please do not hesitate to

contact me if I may of any further assistance.
Yours sincerely,
Dr. Stan Martin
Chair, Pharmaceutical Research Division
National Research Council of Canada

NARRATOR: We set out for Canada, an adventure my parents
             expected to last for two years.

Back at funeral home. Voices in background.

The night before the funeral, I spend hours looking
through my father's photographs, remembering the
journey to Canada and our first years in a new
country.

Music: "The Journey."

Click of camera and sound of flash.

Snapshots from 1958. Memories stand still in my
father's hand-developed sepia and black and white
photos. In his home movies.

*Click of camera. Sound of movie camera-film
winding. Father's voice.*

Here, I am travelling across the world with my
parents, the Sirdar's daughter in my tiny frocks, the
red smocked dress my mother made for me, riding
camels in Egypt, double-decker buses in London.

*Buses in London, British conductor's voice-tour
guide. "Now to your right you have the Tower of
London. Here is Buckingham Palace."*

In Rome, the nuns and priests bless me, call me little
Madonna.

Italian voices—priests, nuns, blessing child.

In Canada, the old photographs catch the scenes,
freeze frames of Kodachrome moments.

Click of camera, film winding.

There we are, the three of us on Parliament Hill among the tulips, my mother in her saris, her Kashmiri shawls, red shoes, red handbag, my father with his turban, me in my British duffle coat with the pointed hood, blue like the one Paddington bear wore.

Camera click, film winding.

In this snapshot I am walking with my mother in the Gatineau Hills in the flame of maple trees. We are dressed to match the countryside, my mother in an orange printed sari and me in my orange dress sashed at the back.

Crunch of autumn leaves underfoot—loud crackling at first, then softer and going under as narrator speaks.

Sound of voices laughing (adults and children), waves, splashing on shoreline, picnic sounds, eating, coke bottles being opened.

MOTHER: Lunch is ready. Everyone come and eat.

Soft sound of water splashing on shoreline.

NARRATOR: Here is a hand-tinted photo. Those aqua-tinted clothes and rosy cheeks. My mother in her 50s bathing suit, posing in front of the rounded curves of our blue Ford. Coke bottles are cooling in the sand, lined up along the shoreline.

Mother and young girl laughing.

Another snapshot—my mother in her pedal pushers, me in my frock and cardigan and red Mary Jane shoes, box of animal crackers dangling from my hands. My mother is beautiful. We are smiling.

I am the only child then. I am home in Canada and beloved.

Music: "The Journey" —out.

Childhood

Resume reading of letter from National Research Council.

NARRATOR: In Ottawa, we live in an international community of scientists with families from many cultures and countries. Whenever my father's friends travel they bring me back gifts from countries I have never seen. I become a collector of beautiful things—the treasures they bring me—dolls in ethnic costumes from around the world, ornate tortoise-shell hair-combs, Spanish castanets...

After our two years in Ottawa, my father is offered a job with Ayerst Pharmaceuticals in Montreal. So we never return to India to live. Canada becomes home. We move to Beaconsfield on the West Island, a white Anglophone community.

As a child, I speak Hindi and Punjabi and English. Soon I learn French. Gradually after my two sisters are born, English becomes the main language of my home and I start to lose my Indian languages.

In Beaconsfield, we are the only Indian family. My mother is an exotic bird, her fashionable western clothes, brilliant saris, her radiant smile. My turbanned, bearded father has his share of encounters with landlords who tell him to go back to where he came from.

I notice my father's difference through other children's eyes.

LITTLE BOY: *(Background.)* Mom, mom, look at that man with the beard and the red hat—is that Santa Claus?

Street noises, traffic. People walking on sidewalks.

Christmas carolers singing "Silent Night", "Deck the Halls."

NARRATOR: We celebrate Christmas in Canada. My sisters and I learn the words to Christmas carols. We learn about magic through my father.

> *Cars driving by on city streets—traffic in winter— sounds of tires crunching on snow, horns blasting, sound of Salvation Army bells collecting for Christmas charity.*

In my memory, my father stands for hours with his little girls in front of Ogilvy's department store on St. Catherine's Street. Ogilvy's wrapped their customers' purchases in green tartan boxes and bags and they had a bagpiper and a tearoom in those years. Ogilvy's was renowned for their amazing Christmas displays, complete with moving elves and toy-making scenes. This year I am remembering, there is a Santa's village display. We stand holding our father's hands in the bitter cold, our breath frosting the air, watching the elves hammering and packing Santa's bag with toys, loading it onto the sleigh with sauntering reindeer, red-nosed Rudolph in the lead. My father fed our dreams and wishes and belief in imagination. He gave us magic.

> *Music: "A little girl's memory of a faraway geography...under my fingernails the scents of spices and teas...the silk phrasings of my mother's saris..." under...*

Postcolonial Lessons

MOTHER: *(Reading to small child.)* Once upon a time there lived in a certain village a pretty country girl. *(Clear at first then voice goes soft under.)*

NARRATOR: I love to hear my mother and father reading to me. Enid Blyton, Kipling, Wordsworth's daffodils... *A Child's Garden of Verses, Arabian Nights, Grimm's Fairy Tales, Little Red Riding Hood,* Rapunzel letting

down her hair...primers of Dick, Jane, Sally, Puff
and Spot, neighbourhoods of sunshine.

I learn every word of *Little Red Riding Hood* by heart.
There is something about that red cloaked spirit that
I love.

NARRATOR'S
POETIC VOICE: Every morning my mother would
part my hair down the middle, plait
it into long braids reaching down to
my waist. I would walk with the other
neighbourhood kids to Briarwood Elementary
School, absent-minded, my face always
in a book, reading as I walked, dressed like
the other girls in dark navy tunics, white blouses,
novitiate-like collars.

Those days, my knees were always scraped
and skinned from roller-skating on the concrete
slopes of Avondale Road, my skate-keys around my
neck, flying, weightless
my father continuously swabbing my cuts
with hydrogen peroxide, scabs peeking out over the
tops of my white kneesocks, my Oxford shoes.[3]

Children singing "God Save the Queen."

In the classroom, we stood at attention
spines stiffened to the strains of singing
God Save the Queen to the Union Jack
recited The Lord's Prayer
hallowed be thy name, learned lessons
from a Gideon's bible.

In geography and history lessons
the teacher would unroll the giant map
of the world from the ceiling, use her
wooden pointer to show us the countries
of the Empire, the slow spread of a faded
red stain that marked them, soft burgundy
like the colour of my father's turbans.
Ancient history. Crisp whites of cricket

matches at officers' clubs. Afternoon tea
in the pavilion.

Decades later I can reconstruct the
story, move past the pink glow,
excavate the hollows of history.

I know now that if that surface was scratched
the pointer would fly along the contours of
the parchment world, across the Himalayas, through
emerald coils of steaming rivers.
Under my fingernails, the scents of spices
and teas, the silk phrasings of my mother's
saris, the stench of imperial legacy, blood
spilled from swords on proper khaki uniforms
lanced through the bodies of Sikh soldiers at
the frontlines of her Majesty's British Army.
But our teacher never said. *Remember this.*[4]

Music fades out.

Voices from TV and radio advertising from the late
50s and early 60s, cheery style slogans with singing
and background music—for example Pepsodent—
"You'll wonder where the yellow went, when you
brush your teeth with Pepsodent..." section ends with
slogan "Things go better with Coke."

NARRATOR: I watch my mother read *Ladies Home Journal* and *Miss*
Chatelaine. Pictures of women with cinch-waist
dresses, bouffant hairdos. They ride in convertibles
with their headscarves keeping every hair in place.
On the domestic front, these women are so happy
with their pink and aqua kitchen appliances. And in
one ad for Scott toilet paper, the woman in the ad
wears an evening gown in the exact pastel blue of the
toilet paper and Kleenex tissue.

The women my mother and I see in these magazines
use Yardley Lavender and Cashmere Bouquet
talcum powder. They buy new davenports and
credenzas. Pictured in exotic landscapes in their

underwear, they dream in their Maidenform bras
and girdles that promise to set them free. I like the
ad for the black lace lingerie called a Merry Widow.
Under the sedate hairdo and perfect makeup of the
model, her Max Factor red lips, this underwear has
a wildness to it I can relate to—some promise of real
excitement.

> *Soft music under narrator's voice—some blend of
> Indian/Persian/Western—sense of soft mystery to
> it—variation on Prelude theme.*

NARRATOR'S
POETIC VOICE: My teachers and the women in the
neighbourhood would admire the crimson
blooms on my mother's Kashmiri shawls,
exotic, intricate embroideries on fine
wool the colour of blackest nightfall.

I know they could never imagine,
as I have only just begun to imagine,
my mother's lost places, her girlhood, the
laughter in summer houses, wild monkeys
at the hill stations of her youth, peacocks,
the heady profusions of flowers and fruit, jasmine
and roses and custard-apples and
guavas. They could not imagine her with
braids and proper Catholic uniform at the
convent school under the stern eyes of nuns
like Sister Mary Joseph and the other sisters
wearing their gleaming Bride of Christ wedding
rings who taught them all the subjects a
    colonial girl should know
including domestic skills such as the tatting of lace
and embroidery stitching.

They could not imagine this, nor could they taste
the sweetness of Sanskrit poetry, or the star-flung
nights of Persian ghazals.[5]

> *Music fading to silence here.*

In Canada, my mother's young life gets frozen into the
icy winters of my childhood, new stories spun
in English on skating rinks, tobogganing hills and
ski slopes. A new wife, a new mother, she reads
Ladies' Home Journal, learns to bake me birthday
cakes and gingerbread houses, wears Western clothes,
pedal pushers and sheath dresses and high heels, sews
me party frocks with sashes bowed in the back.[6]

> *Girl Guides meeting. Voices of guides reciting promise in
> unison, then fading.*

NARRATOR: My mother was a Girl Guide in India. The doctrines of
Lord and Lady Baden-Powell are ever-present in
Canada and so, I am enrolled in Girl Guides. We learn to
recite the Girl Guide promise:

> *Girl Guides' voices reciting again. Voices should be
> prepubescent, slightly out of sync, some louder voices
> competing, off key, some humour to this.*

I promise, on my honour, to do my best:
To do my duty to God, the Queen, and my country,
To help other people at all times,
To obey the Guide Law.

We learn the language of semaphore, how to
build campfires and lean-tos and latrines.
We earn badges, pitch tents, learn how to use an axe
and chop wood,
how to tie knots, learn first aid and how to survive in the
wilderness. We learn to *Be Prepared* and to *Lend a Hand*.

We learn the Guide Law. [7]

> *Girl Guides' voices reciting in unison....under.*

*A Guide is obedient. You obey orders given you by those in
authority, willingly and quickly. Learn to understand that
orders are given for a reason, and must be carried out without
question.*

A Guide smiles and sings even under difficulty. You are

cheerful and willing even when things seem to be going
wrong. A Guide is pure in thought, word and deed. You
look for what is beautiful and good in everything, and try to
become strong enough to discard the ugly and unpleasant.[8]

    "The Day is Done" under...

We became capable girls, soldiers in our uniforms,
    with our companies and patrols and salutes.
We learned to build nations and
at the close of the day, we sing Taps, the
    soldiers' bugle call to
extinguish the lights.[9]

    Girl Guides' voices singing Taps at close of meeting.
    Guide Leader might be introduced as voice calling
    meeting to close.

Day is done, gone the sun
From the hills, from the lake
From the sky
All is well, safely rest
God is nigh.

And our mothers kept house, did the laundry and
the cooking and the ironing, drove us to Brownies
and Girl Guides, did volunteer work,
    refinished furniture,
watched *Another World.* [10]

    Music: "The Day is Done"—out.

    TV beginning of "Another World" soap opera fading
    to sound under following NARRATOR's section.

Mothers and wives took Valium when their lives did
not resemble the glamorous adventures of
Rachel and Mac Corey. Mothers and wives had
hysterectomies at forty.[11]

    "Another World" music fades to silence.

    Mothers' voices calling children in for supper.

"Jimmy, Alan, Debbie...time to come in now. Supper's ready." Cars driving into driveways, car doors opening and closing. Men's shoes tapping on pavement.

At the close of every day, they had supper ready
when their husbands returned from the city,
fresh and slick, briefcases in hand, polished shoes
tapping them home past
manicured lawns along the asphalt driveways.[12]

"The Dance of the Sugar Plum Fairies"...under.

Skiers—swooshing through powdered snow/ski-hill sounds.

For our new Canadian winters, my mother knits us ski sweaters, heavy cable knits that I wear to the local skating rink and to the ski hills. My father learns to ski, a rare sight on the hills of the Eastern Townships, St. Sauveur, Mont Tremblant, his turban and ski goggles, among a sea of white faces in Montreal winters. The newspaper photographs him, writes a story on the Sikh skier in Canada—the new Canadian. Every Saturday morning in winter, he drives me to catch the bus to my ski lessons, picks me up at the end of the day at the Beaconsfield Shopping Centre.

A curious mix, my cultural education. I'm not raised on Indian dance or music but on chamber music concerts, ballets. Every Christmas, my mother dresses me and my sisters in velvet dresses she sews for us, takes us to see the Nutcracker at Place des Arts. And every year those unforgettable ballet classes. The stern Miss Damrol's ballet classes, our pristine white tunics, powder blue sashes, pink tights, at the school gym or Stewart Hall, bodies stiff at the barre, our hair in tight buns at the napes of our necks.

MISS
DAMROL: *(Very formal, British, clipped orders.)* Eyes forward.
               Young ladies, chin up, stomachs in, bottoms tucked,
               plié, port de bras, 1ˢᵗ position, 2ⁿᵈ position, hold it…

NARRATOR: In Beaconsfield, in the late 1960s and early 70s, we
               were more interested in other forms of dancing.

               Late 60s, early 70s rock—Iron Butterfly,
               Steppenwolf…

               Party, rock music, door bell ringing at intervals,
               voices, beer bottles opening, soft hum of voices.

           There we are in a house like all the others,
           freshly painted trim and gabled windows,
                   brass-numbered door
           and neatly pruned hedges, parents away for the
           weekend and the basement recreation room
                   is overflowing
           with us, sweet sixteens, bodies clutched
                   together in sweat
           in the cigarette smoke and beer, slow dancing to
                   Chicago's *Color My World*…[13]

               Brief track from Chicago's "Color My World."

           …and then there was the long drawn out Led
           Zeppelin's *Stairway to Heaven*—the best make out
           and slow dance music because it went on forever.

               Brief track from Zeppelin's "Stairway To Heaven."

           My girlfriends and I wear angora sweaters
                   our mothers
           bought for us in the soft pastel shades of infants:
                   fingernail
           pink, baby blue, pale yellow, and cream.
                   We wear drugstore
           scents named for innocence and fruit:
                   Love's Baby Soft, Love's Fresh
           Lemon, or the more sophisticated *Eau de Love* or
           Revlon's *Charlie*.[14]

> *Music: "The Dance of the Sugar Plum Fairy"—soft under following.*

MISS
DAMROL: Now girls, plié, jetté, first position, second position, hold it…

NARRATOR: For years we have danced in ballet studios,
    spinning, dreaming our
mothers' dreams of Sugar Plum Fairies, our rose
    tight confections, pink
slippers twirling pas de deux, jetés, pirouetting our
    taut muscles until our
toes bled.[15]

> *Music: Cream's "Layla"—soft under NARRATOR's voice following.*

But tonight, we dance in our tight blue Levis, our
    mothers' voices fading
as the shiver of Eric Clapton's electric guitar
    strums our spines, the
music claiming us and we spill out under the
    streetlamps, dancing across
equators into the earth's light.

On the streets of suburbia, this is the beginning of
    hunger.
It catches me by surprise, exploding like a kiss.[16]

> *"Layla"—loud-electric guitar riff-section could play for a while.*

Teenagehood and Reading Like a Girl

> *Music: "Bollywood Billboards" under.*

NARRATOR: Teenagehood. My black hair, olive skin, non typical features. By Indian standards I am fair, a whiteness about me. I speak fluent French and English. In Quebec I am taken for every nationality, Italian, French, Arab, Egyptian. Where are you from? becomes a repeated refrain.

On our first trip to India with my family, this is mirrored in Bollywood billboards, the actresses have dyed their hair reddish brown, their skin is fair. In Indian magazines, feminine beauty ads market skin bleaches to make the skin fair.

Indian Relatives. Under: Some Punjabi voices of women here, mixed with English expressions, enough to convey meaning and translation—to represent aunties commenting on skin color and appearance of the Canadian nieces.

My relatives call me beautiful, fair. They call my darker skinned younger sister *kali*—dark black, less marriageable, less marketable.

Women's Punjabi voices mixed with English.

I feel the guilt of this even then at sixteen, this within culture racism aimed at women's beauty, a woundedness that moves beyond immigrant identity.

Sounds of community swimming pool—kids laughing, splashing, diving into water, sound of diving boards, life guard whistles.

Back in Canada, my girlfriends Colleen, Debbie, Lorrie and I still baste ourselves in baby oil at the Beaconsfield Swimming Pool, seeking Coppertone tans, the white lines at the edges of our bathing suits, the beginning of a sensuous existence of teenage girls.

Sometimes my sister and I dream of being blonde and blue-eyed like the models in *Seventeen* magazine.

In school, we have a special subject designed to help us learn all about our teenage selves.

Music: "Things Will Make Us Bleed" under...

NARRATOR'S
POETIC VOICE: In the 1960s they called it *Health Education*
on our report cards. Today they call the subject
Family Life.
At our school, the girls are separated from
the boys, gathered in the school gymnasium.
The nurse distributes pamphlets about
life cycles and Kotex. There is something
pristine and sanitized about it, the glossy brochures
with the beautiful fresh-faced
girl, her blonde hair swept back with pink
satin ribbon. We know we will soon become
her, young women leading Breck girl lives.

We learn our lessons well, believe we can
hold on to our well-groomed dreams.

It takes us years before we realize how many things
will make us bleed, how easy it is
for the world to rip us to pieces.[17]

> *French children's voices, taunting. Little girl crying.*

> *Music: "Things Will Make Us Bleed"—out.*

NARRATOR: My sister is the first child from Anglophone
Beaconsfield to attend French school. My parents
thought it would be the best way for her to learn
French. She comes home weeping one day from
French school. The French kids call her nigger.

MOTHER: *(Sound of girl crying softly under.)* It's alright, *beta*.
They just don't understand. It's alright to be
different. They don't know any better.

NARRATOR: We do not attend a *Gurudwara*, a Sikh temple, on a
regular basis—only if there was a wedding or
special occasion. My father did not believe in
organized religion. But he was a spiritual man who
lived his life according to humanist principles. So in
sixties fashion, my parents took us to a Unitarian
church in Pointe Claire. In 1967, the minister was

Fred Cappuccino. With his wife Bonnie, they had two birth children and many adopted children from around the world.

Sound tracks from "Reach For The Top" under...

At Beaconsfield High School, I am on the debate team, the "Reach for the Top" quiz show team, a bit of a geek but still popular in a way that enables me to have a sense of a secret identity. My mother's refrain at this time of my life is: Don't talk so much, a girl should be more reserved. She wanted me to excel at everything, be strong but reserved, articulate but quiet...

She wanted me to have a profession she could define—lawyer, doctor, teacher, engineer, something that has a label. I never imagined I would become a poet but years later she gives me a tiny notebook she had saved. I had written it when I was twelve- descriptive, flowery nature poems, full of allusions to classical myth.

Music: "Wonder Woman Was Beautiful"...under.

NARRATOR'S
POETIC VOICE: Oh how I loved books! I devoured them, eating up the words, glorying in the fictional lives of characters. In these years I walked around in an absent-minded haze, immersed in these other worlds I was reading about. I read while getting dressed, eating meals, walking to school. And how I loved comic books!

The comic book heroes I loved best
were the mutants and freaks.
Spiderman and Batman, Aquaman who was half-
    fish and
of course Superman who could be mistaken for a
        bird or a plane.

And then there was Wonder Woman. She was
    glorious,

descended from the Amazons of Greek myth. She had
fabulous breasts and a magic lasso and belt
as well as those bulletproof wristbands worn by the
Amazons to remind them of the folly of submitting
      to men's domination.

Wonder Woman was beautiful and powerful as a hero,
understated and reserved in her secret identity as Diana
Prince,
the secretary in her smart chic glasses.

What the superheroes taught me was unintentional
radical truth. The geek and hybrid mutant was a
      treasure,
so easily misunderstood in real life so
a secret identity

                              was necessary.
This I took to heart.
And how I loved the other girls and women in
      my novels:
How I loved them, the stories about the
girl detectives, spunky and brave, solving
crimes with their wits and brains and
All-American good looks. Long after my
mother thought I was asleep, late into the
night, I would read under the covers with
a flashlight.

I drove that blue roadster with Nancy
Drew, dated Ned, and looked lovely and
charming
and desirable at college football games.

And how I dreamed of being Cherry Ames, student
nurse, with her stylish cap and uniform, her black hair
and rosy cheeks, her boyfriends and her
adventures.

And when I grew up, I became them, Nancy and
Cherry.
I cut off my long black braids, styled my hair
      into a bob.

I became the girl detective, the nurse, capable of
    building
nations and soothing the hearts of men. I became
    Nancy and
Cherry, for awhile.

Music "Wonder Woman Was Beautiful"...out.

*Sounds of cheerleaders chanting at football game,
football game sounds on field.*

NARRATOR'S
POETIC VOICE: On the autumn football fields
the cheerleaders chant and jump
their pleated miniskirts flipped into the air,
flurries of thighs gleaming.
Anything seems possible, for such
young bodies, in such a place and
time.

I remain reading my books under the
trees, losing myself in imaginary
worlds, in the tomes of *War and Peace*
and *Dr. Zhivago*, dreaming of dancing in
evening gowns and elbow-length gloves. Books
about revolution excited me,
seduced me.

I try to re-imagine the heroines,
their perpetual tragedies.
Emma Bovary, Anna Karenina.
Anna flinging her body into the locomotive steam,
her red purse on the tracks. I try to read them and
write them differently, give them different endings,
new destinies.

I want them to stay alive, to breathe, to be
plump with blood and desire, to believe that
anything is possible.

Music: Short sound bites from Jimi Hendrix.

NARRATOR: The late 1960s were rebel years when my parents

waited up for me at night, smelled my breath for traces of alcohol.

Car door opening. Girl kissing boy goodnight. Fumbling. Adolescent boy's voice moaning: Mmm, you feel so good.

TEENAGE
VOICE OF
NARRATOR: OK. I gotta go. My mother's waiting up for me.

Car door slamming, driving away. House door opening.

MOTHER: Where have you been? What have you been doing? It's so late...

NARRATOR
(*Adult Voice*):   My mother would run her hands across my back to make sure I was wearing a bra. She would check the length of my skirts as I left the house. I wore miniskirts, rolled up the waistbands after I left home to make them even shorter...I wore hotpants and fishnets. My mother stopped smiling in these years—told me I should be modest and show no cleavage.

The Raj Kumari Leaves Home

Sound of phone ringing/answering machine:

VOICE OF
NARRATOR
(*age 18*):   Hi, I can't come to the phone right now. Leave a message.

NARRATOR: I left Beaconsfield to study literature, languages and translation at University at 18. I met Jay, a young man from New Brunswick. He is long limbed and lean and sweet. I am in love.

Ringing of phone. Click to answering machine.

VOICE OF
NARRATOR
(*age 18*):   Hi, I can't come to the phone right now. Leave a
                     message.

                     Beep of answering machine.

MOTHER: *Beta*, We can never reach you. You're never home.
                     Are you studying? Call us back.

                     *Tone at end of mother's message. Click, hanging up
                     of phone.*

                     Phone ringing. Click to answering machine.

VOICE OF
NARRATOR
(*age 18*):   Hi, I can't come to the phone right now. Leave a
                     message.

                     Beep of answering machine.

MOTHER: *Beta*, What are you doing? Your uncle wrote from
                     India some eligible men London—*Angreji* educated
                     who want to marry and come to Canada. One is an
                     engineer and one a doctor—good families and
                     good-looking boys. (*She gives big sigh, exasperated,
                     then tsk, tsk sound.*)

                     You are becoming too Western. You should
                     remember your culture. Love you. Call us.

                     *Tone at end of message. Sound of message
                     rewinding.*

NARRATOR: I come home for the summer after my first year at
                     university. It is the time of the referendum in
                     Quebec.

                     *Sound clips from Quebec news broadcasts and
                     newspaper headlines—French and English, during
                     this time, conflict about sign laws—create some
                     sense of danger, instability, threat to the known life.*

My neighbourhood has been vandalized. I am shocked by the stop-signs with the word STOP slashed out with black paint, the word ARRÉT written over top. Everywhere, there is a war of language on our neighbourhood signs. Langue, ma langue. In French, the same word for tongue. I always thought French and English were my languages, mes langues, my tongues, the tongues of home.

My mother finds my birth control pills, calls me a prostitute. I move into an apartment with Jay. My parents are beside themselves with worry. After several years of living together I phone home.

Phone ringing.

MOTHER: Hello?

NARRATOR: Hi Mom. It's me.

MOTHER: How are you? Are you alright? How come you haven't returned my phone calls?

NARRATOR: *(Silence for a while, sighs of frustration.)* Mom, Jay and I want to get married and we want a civil ceremony at City Hall with a Justice of the Peace.

MOTHER: *(Silence for a bit. Then angry, tight, clipped voice.)* Well if you want to do that your father and I will not attend your wedding.

NARRATOR: My mother refuses to meet Jay. She talks to him on the phone after some coaxing but never physically meets him until the wedding. Jay and I decide we will have the wedding my parents want—they can send photos to the relatives in India and make everyone happy.

The Wedding

Wedding music resolves into the Anand Raj chant…

People bustling around, swish of silk, soft voices.

NARRATOR: August 18, 1979. We end up having a Sikh wedding
and a United Church wedding. The night before the
wedding, my hands are painted with *mehndi*, in
intricate designs of henna. The day of the wedding I
realize I can't dress myself. My aunts have to wrap
and fold and drape my sari around my body. My
wedding sari is not the usual bridal red. I have
rebelled against the red brocade encrusted heavy
wedding saris. My sari is pale peach-pink, a shot
silk like dawn with a deep purple and gold brocade
border. I wear a pale mauve orchid in my black hair.
In traditional ceremonies, the groom rides up on a
white horse but we dispensed with this custom. Jay
wears a turban and my mother begins to love him a
little.

> *Music/Chant of Anand Karaj—Sikh holy prayers
> and wedding ceremony in background. Singing of
> Prayers—"Kirtan"—hymns from Sikh holy book
> composed in Indian classical style. Music and
> prayers fading to background under following.*

NARRATOR: The *Anand Karaj*, the Sikh wedding ceremony
begins. I am laden with gold—a *rani-haar*-necklace
around my throat, my hands painted in henna
designs—the bridal *mehndi*—head covered and
suitably bowed, the Sirdar's daughter.

During the *Anand Karaj*, to signify our union and the
giving away of the bride, my father places one end
of a scarf in my hand and the other in Jay's hands.
The *Adi Granth*, the holy book, is opened and *Lavan*,
the marriage prayers are read. During each of the
four stanzas, we walk around the holy book. Still
holding our ends of the scarf, we circle around the
book four times. I am guided by men, my groom,
my father, cousin, uncle, as if I could not find my
way.

> *Anand Sahib—short prayer said before final prayer.
> Hukam, the day's lesson from the scripture.*

At the end of the ceremony we are given *Kara Parshad*—a holy sweet to share with the congregation. We sign the register, Jay takes off his turban and then we are married again in a Christian ceremony.

Reverend's voice reading marriage service of the United Church.

We are double-ringed. I see the look of relief on my mother-in-law's face as she hears the English vows she understands.

Music: "Soja Lullaby Variation" under...

Then there is the garlanding ceremony. As we leave the church my parents and relatives necklace us with flower garlands to bless us and congratulate us. We are showered with rose petals.

At the end of the day, I look over at Jay, my sisters, mother, father, everyone dancing, all beloved, all strangers.

Princess Diaries

NARRATOR: When my first child is born, my first daughter, my father builds her a pine cradle. It is painstaking labor to build it. He sends it in pieces with my mother who comes to visit while I am still in the hospital. Along with it he sends a letter:

FATHER &
NARRATOR
(Together):   My dearest: I remember clearly the day you were born. Now you have a daughter of your own. I wish I could be with you now but will join you soon and in the meantime I have sent directions with your mother on how to put together the cradle for my new granddaughter. I don't think I have ever put so much into creating something even for you girls as I have on this cradle. Please send me photos of Cara sleeping in it when you can...

NARRATOR: Every Sikh girl is named *Kaur*, meaning princess—it is her name along with her other given names.

NARRATOR'S
POETIC VOICE: When I was young my father called me *Princess*. And princess stories were the ones I loved most, especially the one about Sleeping Beauty. Her name was sometimes Briar Rose or Aurora. The story of the beautiful princess who pricked her finger on the spindle of a spinning wheel, falling under the spell of the witch who had been shunned at her christening.

The curse of a girlchild's birth. She slept along with the kingdom for a hundred years
until she is rescued by a handsome prince who hacked
through the dense tangle of thorns and wild rose bushes.
The curse lifted with love, his kiss on her lips,
awakening the world.

When my daughters are young, I read them princess stories
The Paper Bag Princess, *The Princess and the Motorcycle*.
Tales of strong, independent princesses
of wit and courage and
intellect who do not depend on princes for survival.

Still, as I watch my girls, young women now, I am filled
with longing, something that mourns the loss of belief
that a beloved would hack through forests of
thorns to
sweep a girl off her feet.[18]

Music: "Soja Variation" ends…

Harry Belafonte singing "Jamaica Farewell" under…

NARRATOR: The question of language always haunts me, brings me back to a memory of a lover who wanted to know about my childhood, my childhood language. He wanted to know my father's words, called me *beta*, little one, child, my father's name for me, as he stroked my hair back from my forehead. And in these moments I realized how much of this language was deeply connected to a place of soul for me. Punjabi-there is still something beloved about this tongue. Some sense of home, like the poem, a shelter we make of words...

Soja

Sound of someone cooking in kitchen...food frying, stirring of pot, clink of kitchen utensils, etc. MOTHER singing or humming to Belafonte in kitchen.

NARRATOR: In my memory it is May 25, 1990. My father is 62 years old. My mother and father have many plans for his retirement in a few years, travels around the world. My mother now works at the Beaconsfield Public Library. He leaves my mother cooking dinner.

Couple kissing and embracing.

FATHER: Rani, *(In Punjabi and English.)* I'm just going for a quick game of tennis.

MOTHER: *Acha*, allright, come home soon.

NARRATOR: He goes to the Pointe Claire Tennis Club for a game with a close friend.

Tennis court sounds...balls, rackets hitting balls, balls thudding on clay courts.

NARRATOR: A blood clot finds its way into his heart and he dies instantly there on the red earth courts.

Phone ringing.

MOTHER: Hello?

WOMAN'Ss
VOICE
(on telephone):   Mrs. Singh?

MOTHER: Yes?

Music is stopped.

NARRATOR: My mother is still cooking when she gets the call
            from the Lakeshore General Hospital. Life is never
            quite the same. We mourn, we gleam.

Music: "In My Mother's House..." under...

NARRATOR'S
POETIC VOICE: In my mother's house
             the scent of memory lives,
             in the French perfumes he gave her,
             Chanel No.5, Miss Dior,
             the rounded glass bottle of Worth's *Je Reviens,*
             lingerie drawers of lace and fragrant silks,
             lush bouquets of anniversaries.

             Everywhere, photographs imprint
             our surfaces, lives stilled in sepia
             and Kodachrome.

             I know the gleam and smell of
             the polished leather of his shoes, buffed
             every morning before he left for work.
             I press my face into the crisp white
             cotton of his shirts, brush my cheek against
             his jackets, his sweaters, still warm with the
             smell of him. I touch my teeth to the metal
             of his watch, his cufflinks.

             I can hear his voice reading fairytales,
             singing the calypso of Harry Belafonte,
             crooning Punjabi ghazals and lullabies

             Soja Rajkumari, soja,
             Sleep, little princess, sleep
             Soja meethe sapne aayen
             Sleep with sweet dreams
             Soja pyari Rajkumari
             Sleep beloved princess [19]

In the hush, I am cradled by
the sound of him, notes love-woven,
tangled through the glowing pyre.

In my mother's house
my father's ashes are acrid
in my throat.

And everywhere I travel in life there is still this—
A small girl in her red smocked dress,
her red Mary Janes.
Her father clasps her hand in his, teaches her
to recognize the convulsive beauty of things...[20]

> *Sound effect: Return to funeral home, sounds of
> voices in background.*

NARRATOR: May 28, 1990. And here I am in Beaconsfield again.
Kissing my father's forehead before we let him go to
the crematorium. How the return home can be
treacherous, unstable in its memories. And in the
end immigrants and others in the world we call
home must invent a history of shared space to dwell
in. And I in my blue sari will one day help my
mother and my sisters to spread my father's ashes
on the waters of the lake he loved, in the place we
called home.

> *Music: "In My Mother's House" up and hold for
> credits...*

The End.

Endnotes

[1]   Dunlop, Rishma. "Ancestors." *Red Silk*: *An Anthology of Canadian South Asian Women Poets*. Toronto: Mansfield Press, 2004.

[2]   Dunlop, Rishma. "Ancestors." *Red Silk*.

[3]   Dunlop, Rishma. "First Lessons: Postcolonial." *Reading Like a Girl*. Windsor: Black Moss Press, 2004, p. 30.

[4]   Dunlop, Rishma. "First Lessons: Postcolonial."

[5]   Dunlop, Rishma. "My Mother's Lost Places." *Reading Like a Girl*. Windsor: Black Moss Press, 2004, p. 32.

[6]   Dunlop, Rishma. "My Mother's Lost Places."

[7]   Dunlop, Rishma. "The Education of Girls." *Reading Like a Girl*, p. 33.

[8]   Excerpts from the Guide Law, Guide Promise and Guide Motto are from *The Guide Handbook*, Girl Guides of Canada, First Edition, 1965, pp.6-10.

[9]   "The Education of Girls," p. 33.

[10] "The Education of Girls," p. 33.

[11] "The Education of Girls," p. 33.

[12] "The Education of Girls," p. 33.

[13] Dunlop, Rishma. "Slow Dancing: Beaconsfield, 1973." *Reading Like a Girl*, p. 41.

[14] "Slow Dancing."

[15] "Slow Dancing."

[16] "Slow Dancing."

[17] Dunlop, Rishma. "Reading Like a Girl: 4." *Reading Like a Girl*, p. 38.

[18] Dunlop, Rishma. "Princess Stories." *Reading Like A Girl*, p. 42.

[19] Dunlop, Rishma. "Soja." *Reading Like a Girl*, p. 43-44

[20] Dunlop, Rishma. "Gathering Lilacs." *Reading Like a Girl*, p. 17.

Crossing Gibraltar

(The Parallel Lives of Bassel)

Ehab Lotayef

Ehab Lotayef

Born in Cairo, Egypt in 1958, Lotayef graduated from the Faculty of Engineering at Ain Shams University in his birth city, in 1981. He emigrated to Canada in 1989 and now lives and works in Montreal, where he is a Computers Systems Manager at McGill. He balances his day job with many literary and theatrical pursuits; as a poet and songwriter he works in both Arabic and English, writes Haiku, and is a performer and member of Montreal's Teesri Duniya Theatre.

About the Play

Crossing Gibraltar explores a question that every immigrant has at one point or another asked himself—what would his life be had he changed his mind at the crucial moment before emigrating, and remained in his native country?

Bassel left his life in Cairo in the 1980s, and came to Montreal, where he slowly adapted to Canadian culture. We follow his loves and life through to the terrible events of September 11, 2001, and come to an understanding through Bassel of the contradictions, tribulations and joy of being a man of Arab descent in Canada...

But what if Bassel had gotten cold feet at Cairo airport, and not made that fateful decision to leave his homeland? Ehab Lotayef also explores the life of Bassel who stayed in Cairo, and how living in that country over the past twenty years has given him a different perspective on world events.

Bassel's story parallels in some respects that of author Lotayef.

Cast

BASSEL: .... Shant Srabian

SALAH: .... Frazad Sadrian

SELEEM: .... Mike Haddad

LAILA: .... Rahnuma Panthaky

HÉLÈNE: .... Carolyne Maraghi

PAUL: .... Billly Khoury

STAN: .... Alex Coury

SALWA: .... Laila Moos

SARA/MEMORIAL GIRL: .... Nadia Mansouri

JIM: .... Michael Badaway

Characters

BASSEL: .... b. 1957, dual main character

SALAH: .... b. 1945, casual encounter

SELEEM: .... b. 1958, friend

LAILA: .... b. 1960, wife

HÉLÈNE: .... b. 1962, Francophone girlfriend

PAUL: .... b. 1960, co-worker

STAN: .... b. 1959, friend and co-worker

SALWA: .... b. 1968, project fiancée

SARA: .... b. 1969, wife, Syrian/Quebecois

JIM: .... b. 1978, junior co-worker

Production Credits

Producer/Director: .... Damiano Pietropaolo

Associate Producer: .... Rosie Fernandez

Script Editor: .... Dave Carley

Casting: .... Linda Grearson

Recording Engineer: .... Wayne Richards

Sound Effects: .... Joe Mahoney

Scene Breakdown

Scene 1   Two Bassels debate, September 2001
Scene 2   Cairo Airport, August 1987
Scene 3   Montreal, November 1989
Scene 4   Cairo, November 1989
Scene 5   Montreal, September 1993
Scene 6   Cairo, September 1993
Scene 7   Montreal, April 1995
Scene 8   Cairo, April 1995
Scene 9   Montreal, September 1997
Scene 10 Cairo, September 1997
Scene 11 Montreal, September 11, 2001
Scene 12 Mediterranean resort, September 11, 2001
Scene 13 Montreal, September 11, 2002
Scene 14 Cairo, September 11, 2002

Scene 1
September 11, 2001: Nowhere in Particular

> *Archival CBC radio news. Recount of the events of the day, 9-11—establish then fade to background and hold...*

EGYPTIAN
BASSEL: Psst.
"*Ya*" Mister... Hey you!

CANADIAN
BASSEL: *(Confused.)* Who's that?

E. BASSEL: It's you. I mean me who is you. We're the same person.

C. BASSEL: *(Further confused.)* What?

E. BASSEL: I told you; I'm you and you're me. I'm Bassel.

C. BASSEL: What are you talking about!

E. BASSEL: Forget it. I just want to ask you a question. Would you humour me and answer?

C. BASSEL: Go ahead and ask. Let's get this over with.

E. BASSEL: Do you think they'll really leave you alone now? Do you think you'll live in peace? Will they let you feel at home there, as you always dreamed, after what happened? You're the enemy now, loud and clear.

C. BASSEL: What is it to you?

E. BASSEL: Just answer me. Are you embarrassed to answer?

C. BASSEL: OK. Some won't leave me alone. But it won't be that bad. I'll hear indirect hints. And maybe sometimes

	insults. But I don't think it'll go beyond that. What's this all about anyway?
E. BASSEL:	You left Egypt hoping to find a Utopia. Now it's clear that there is no Utopia. It is clear that you took the wrong decision and I took the right one.
C. BASSEL:	If I would have stayed, where would I be now? What problems would I be facing? Quite a few, no?
E. BASSEL:	So what? At least you wouldn't be the perpetual outsider.
C. BASSEL:	Look, let's not make it about scoring points. Let's try to be objective. Tell me, you who never left Egypt, are you happy?
E. BASSEL:	Are you?

Fades out into the bells in the next scene.

Scene 2
August 9, 1987: Cairo International Airport

	P.A. system—three bells before announcer comes on in Arabic then English with an Egyptian accent. Pong. Pong. Pong. "Egypt Air announces Flight 871 from Cairo to New York. All passengers please proceed to Gate Number 7."
SALAH:	*(To BASSEL.)* Going to America?
BASSEL:	Canada actually. I have a connecting flight from New York to Montreal.
SALAH:	Immigration.
BASSEL:	*(Feeling uncomfortable.)* Yes.
SALAH:	Lucky guy. You are leaving this place with all its problems behind.
BASSEL:	*"Al-hamd-u lil-Lah." (Int.)* I feel less certain I want to do this day after day. But now it's too late anyway.

SALAH: I'm Salah Abou Raya.

BASSEL: I'm Bassel, Bassel Abd-er-Reheem. Are you going to America?

SALAH: Just a short two-week trip. Work assignment and, of course, a long shopping list for the wife, the kids, the mother-in-law, the extended family and friends. Then back...back to reality. But I am lucky enough to get one of these trips every couple of years. Last time was two years ago, in '85, and they were having this big musical Live Aid concert in Philadelphia, where I stayed. It was so crowded. I hope there is nothing going on there now.

BASSEL: I've never been to America.

SALAH: Now you will be there—or close—forever... And the family?

BASSEL: There is no family.

SALAH: Not married?

BASSEL: *(Int.)* Am I too old to be still single? *(Ext.)* I was supposed to get engaged this year...

SALAH: And?

BASSEL: I knew her for two years, a co-worker, but after long discussions I found that she would not be able to cope with the new life. We grew apart very quickly since the immigration idea started to be a reality. We found that we don't really think alike. We decided to end it while still on the shore. No regrets. *(Int.)* Why am I telling him all this?

SALAH: And of course you took a leave of absence from work.

BASSEL: Actually, no. My parents have both passed away. No siblings. So I did what Tareq Ibn Ziad did when he crossed the straight of Gibraltar to Spain. I burnt

	all my ships and now it's the sea behind me and the new life in front of me.

SALAH: That's not prudent. I heard horror stories about people who didn't make it, came back and had to start from scratch. Anyway, good luck. (*Unconvincingly.*) You seem to be a bright guy and things will sure work out for you. (*With a bit of envy.*) May God grant us the same chance, "*Ew'edna ya Rab.*"

BASSEL: That is the only way I know how to do things. I can't be half-hearted about anything I do. I am going to show them that I am as good as any Canadian and I am not going to return defeated. I will succeed. That has to be the only option. It's 1987, I turned 30 this year, I am starting a new life, and—"*in shaa Allah*"— I will succeed.

SALAH: And your religion. You are a Muslim, aren't you?

BASSEL: I am. But what does this have to do with anything? I will continue to be the same Muslim I was here. I did my research and all are equal in Canada. (*Int.*) I'm sounding more confident than I really am. What is wrong with me? Did I take the wrong decision?

SALAH: It may not be that simple. Good luck anyway.

           P.A. system. Three bells before announcer comes on in Arabic then English with an accent. Pong. Pong. Pong. "This is the last call for Egypt Air Flight Number 871 from Cairo to New York is now boarding. All passengers ready for boarding."

           See you in the plane, I like to be at the front of the queue. (*Moves off.*)

BASSEL: Salaam.

           (*Int.*) I can still turn back. Last chance.

           (*Int.*) I'm not getting on that plane.

(Int.) Of course I am. It's not a joke.

(Int.) I'm not leaving.

(Int.) You must be kidding. Turn back now? Keep going.

(Int.) I'm not going.

(Int.) Of course I'm going.

(Int.) I'm not going... Going of course... Not going... Going... Not going... Going... Not going *(Fade out.)*

Scene 3
November 1989: Montreal

> *Crowded and noisy coffee shop in Montreal. Sounds of cups and footsteps, French words in background, loud then fades into popular 1989 Milli Vanilli "Girl You Know it's True" song which itself fades but remains in the background.*

HÉLÈNE: Excuse, je peux avoir le sucre?... Can I have the sugar?

BASSEL: *(Puts down his newspaper—we hear the paper crunching.)* Sure.

HÉLÈNE: Merci.

> *Paper crunching again.*

Do you need it back?

BASSEL: Yes please. I always add more sugar after drinking half the cup. *(Laughs.)*

HÉLÈNE: Too much sugar isn't good for you, you know? I saw how you kept adding sugar to your coffee before I asked you for it. I thought you were not paying attention because you seemed totally absorbed by what you were reading in the paper.

BASSEL: I am fascinated by the fall of the Berlin Wall. Something I never imagined I would live to see. I believed that the age of revolutions is over.

HÉLÈNE: I heard that the people of East Germany were chanting "Gorbie, help us!" I couldn't imagine a Soviet leader being called Gorbie. More like a rock star. *(Sexy laugh.)*

BASSEL: True. Gorbachev is very different from the image we have of Soviet leaders. Who knows what could happen next. But it's all for the better. Communism is no good.

HÉLÈNE: I hope you don't mind if I ask where you come from.

BASSEL: Not at all. I am from Egypt. Immigrated here two years ago.

            Chair scrape.

HÉLÈNE: Je peux m'asseoir? Do you have a communist system in Egypt?

BASSEL: It was sort of socialist till the seventies, when our president, Sadat, opened up to the West and tried to switch to a capitalist economy, but not with very good results. The economy is not doing well.

HÉLÈNE: Why?

BASSEL: Difficult to say, actually. An imported system, not stemming from the people. Corruption in the government. Consumption growing faster than production, much faster. *(Sounds vulnerable.)* Difficult to say.

HÉLÈNE: I hope you are not offended by my questions.

BASSEL: Not at all.

HÉLÈNE: Is Egypt an Islamic country?

BASSEL: Yes, the majority of the population is Muslim. It's a Muslim country.

HÉLÈNE: Maybe that is why it didn't work.

BASSEL: I don't think that has much to do with it. Some people have a closed minded view of religion that may affect progress, but I don't think it's that simple to link the two.

HÉLÈNE: Again, I hope you don't mind, but your religion prohibits women from participating in public life. They can't get education or work. Doesn't this hamper the development of society as a whole?

BASSEL: *(Annoyed, but trying to control it.)* You state these things as if they are facts. My class in university was 50-50 men and women. The image you have is not true. Islam doesn't oppress women, as many like to say.

HÉLÈNE: Je m'excuse. I didn't mean to offend you.

BASSEL: Can I ask you a question?

HÉLÈNE: Sure.

BASSEL: Are you Christian?

HÉLÈNE: My parents were Catholic. Mais pas moi, non. I am beyond this stuff. We have evolved enough to be able to think for ourselves. We don't need a 2,000 year old book to tell us what to do, and what not to do.

BASSEL: There is good in religion.

HÉLÈNE: Not for me. *(Suddenly looks at her watch.)* Ah…je doit m'en allée. Got to go. *(Sipping the last sip of coffee and putting a book in her bag as she talks.)* It would be nice to continue this conversation some other time. I'm Hélène, by the way. *(Laughs.)*

BASSEL: I'm Bassel.

HÉLÈNE: *(She didn't seem to hear him.)* Give me your pen.

                Scribbles something on his newspaper.

HÉLÈNE: Here's my phone number, call me. Bye.

BASSEL: *(She's already walking away.)* Bye. *(Opening his paper slowly.) (Int.)* I'll never understand how they think. *(Pause.) (Int.)* Or maybe I will, one day.

Scene 4
Cairo November 1989

The sound of the Aazaan—Muslim call for prayer—in the background coming that continues throughout a part of the scene.

Door bell rings loud and continuous.

BASSEL: *(Annoyed.)* I'm coming…I'm coming.

SELEEM: *(From behind the door.)* Open up you lazy guy. It's noon.

Door opens, Aazaan still in background.

BASSEL: *Salaam,* Seleem.

SELEEM: *Salaam,* Bassel. How are you? Any of the guys here yet? *(Shocked or faking it.)* Still in your pyjamas?

BASSEL: Slow down. There's no one here yet. It's still early. No one's coming before the Friday prayers. I assume you are not going to pray.

SELEEM: *(Sarcastically.)* I assume you're not going to the prayers either. And I can also assume that you are going to use my presence as an excuse for not going.

BASSEL: *(Int.)* Because I am the only bachelor with his own apartment it becomes the meeting place. *(Ext.)* If I had gone to Canada I wouldn't have had to endure this exercise every Friday. *(Avoiding the discussion.)* Feel at home. I'm going to get dressed.

SELEEM: Make me a cup of tea first. Why hurry. Let's have tea. *"Wahed shaaay sokar zyada law samaht."*

Footsteps behind the next two phrases as they walk to the kitchen. During the conversation we hear various noises, striking a match, water boiling, pouring tea, etc.

BASSEL: So, who's coming?

SELEEM: How would I know? We are the only ones that are always there. The wives control the others. Thank God for being bachelors *"Allahuma deemha neema ya Rab."*

BASSEL: You know very well that you would rather be married, so cut the bullshit.

SELEEM: Freedom man, freedom.

BASSEL: Speaking of freedom, did you hear what is happening in Germany?

SELEEM: In soccer?

BASSEL: No, idiot, the Berlin Wall fell. Communist East Germany is finished. They are now free and Germany will unify. East Germans, after years of communism, are going to join the "real" Europe.

SELEEM: You and your admiration for the West! Why didn't you emigrate to them when you had the chance? You know you never told me why you came back that day. We said goodbye and you went through Immigration. Your luggage was on the plane. Then you came back. Why?

BASSEL: I did tell you. Many times. It's simple. My decision not to leave was the right one. The right one for me. This has nothing to do with admiring or not admiring the West. For the East Germans it sure is better to reunite with the West and become a part of the West.

SELEEM: I want to know what went through your head. You had us all fooled. We didn't see any hesitation on your part. What happened in there? Did you see a ghost? Get a revelation?

BASSEL: Don't be stupid now.

SELEEM: OK, let's be serious. What happened? You seemed so sure. You were always making the analogy with crossing the straight of Gibraltar and burning all your ships behind you. No return. What happened?

BASSEL: *(Serious and very slow, reflecting.)* I don't know. I panicked. I imagined myself jobless and running out of money in a strange city where I know no one. *(Louder.)* Enough please.

SELEEM: OK, OK. I'll let you off the hook now, but one day we'll revisit this.

Moments of silence. Pouring tea.

BASSEL: Rejoining the West is the right thing for the East Germans.

SELEEM: Who says that it's better for them? What has the open market economy done for us? Our pound is about to be three for a dollar. Before the "open economy" it was worth more than a dollar.

BASSEL: That's different.

SELEEM: Why is it different?

BASSEL: Many reasons. We are unable to embrace the Western model in full. We remain stuck in our ways and think that we can get the best of both worlds.

SELEEM: Why can't we be one and the same?

BASSEL: It's a waste of time discussing with you. Let me go get dressed.

SELEEM: We have time. Stop treating me like an idiot just because I don't pretend, like you do, to understand everything. I am as well informed as you are. The West only wants us as a market for their goods and as a source for natural resources and raw materials. We are not—and will never be—a full partner. Any reasons given for our poor economic situation are to disguise these facts. Anwar Sadat did all what they asked for, politically and economically. What more can we do?

BASSEL: It is inside the human being. That's what you don't understand.

SELEEM: *(Sarcastically.)* Inside me! Where? I can't feel anything! *(More serious.)* Cultural differences, my dear, should have nothing to do with it if they are really as democratic, fair, and evolved as they claim to be.

BASSEL: But cultural differences affect everything else. And it is not only that. Look at South East Asia. They are prospering despite having the same cultural differences with the West as we do.

SELEEM: I agree, and disagree. We can do better if we depend on ourselves. That is a part of what is happening in South East Asia. We have problems and we shouldn't blame everything on the West. Still, a couple of hundred years of occupation and imperialist control do leave deep marks.

BASSEL: Yes, they did. The question is how long do we have to wait? Why did Malaysia succeed?

SELEEM: Wait and see, one day the West will turn against them.

BASSEL: Why would they?

SELEEM: You are brainwashed by Western propaganda. Sometimes so brainwashed that you lose your clear logical thinking. You should have emigrated when you had the chance. You are here now and I advise you to accept the world you live in.

BASSEL: Don't start again…

Door bell rings.

...someone's here. Open the door. I'll go get dressed.

Scene 5
Montreal September 1993

Water cooler discussion. Throughout the scene office noises are heard: photocopier, footsteps, etc.

PAUL: Hey Bassel.

BASSEL: *(Much better command of English than in Scene 3.)* Hi Paul.

PAUL: So, what do you think?

BASSEL: About what?

PAUL: About the peace. Signing the Oslo agreement. Finally there is peace in the Middle East. Happy?

BASSEL: It's great, isn't it? *(Doesn't sound convinced.)* I am happy that there is finally a prospect of peace. War has caused so much suffering and hardship over there. And not the least to my old country.

PAUL: Do you think it will last? Do you think 1993 will go down in history as the year peace was established in the Middle East? With all due respect, I think your people love war.

BASSEL: *(Controlling his tone of voice.)* No one wants war, Paul. What can people want more than justice and peace? People—ordinary people—gain nothing from war.

PAUL: Well, some do.

STAN: *(Moving on.)* Hi. What's up?

PAUL: Hello Stan. We're discussing the Middle East. Do you think this peace agreement is the start of something new over there?

STAN: I certainly hope so. What do you think? Are you
                sceptical?

PAUL: I'm not sceptical. I just know better. Got to get back
                to work. *(Moving off.)* Have to leave at five sharp
                today. *(Winks.)* See ya.

STAN: What was that asshole telling you?

BASSEL: Don't worry about it. Very few understand the
                Palestinian problem. They think the Arabs don't
                want peace. I still find this perception very strange.

STAN: I advised you before not to discuss this issue with
                him. Don't even tell him anything. He can cause
                problems. He can misquote you and can get you in
                real trouble. I told you he tried before.

BASSEL: Yes, I know, but I have to explain what I can, when
                I can.

STAN: To those who are ready to listen with an open mind.
                Paul will just choose the parts of what you say that
                confirm his prejudice. On the other hand, the
                majority just don't want to know. They are not
                interested.

BASSEL: I still blame us Arabs to some extent. We don't know
                how to tell our story or win public sympathy,
                especially in the U.S.

STAN: Don't be so tough on your own people. The
                propaganda in the West is sometimes very hard to
                beat. Before I knew you I was the same. Sometimes
                we just can't believe anything that contradicts what
                we grew up knowing.

BASSEL: *(Sighing.)* Anyway. *(Change of tone.)* How is Anne?

STAN: She's well. How are you and Hélène doing? We
                really enjoyed that evening we spent together.

BASSEL: We're doing fine... Well ...

STAN: What?

BASSEL: Nothing much. You know how you just said that it
             is difficult to change the way you look at things you
             grew up with. This is exactly what makes me
             uncertain about any future with Hélène. Although I
             can't deny that she loves me, she wants to change
             me. She has views about Islam, for example, that I
             don't think she will ever change.

STAN: And this affects your relationship? You are in no
             way the "Muslim" we see on TV or hear about in the
             news.

BASSEL: The TV and the news show the worst examples.
             They parade the freaks for entertainment. I,
             although I haven't been in a mosque for years, am
             still a Muslim. I believe in Islam and respect it.

STAN: So where is the problem?

BASSEL: I consider myself a Muslim. I may go to a club and
             drink on occasion, but I am a Muslim. I want to
             define my kids— *(With a sigh.)* if I ever have any—
             as Muslims. Hélène is not even open to discussing
             this. And her political views are sometimes close to
             Paul's.

PAUL: *(Passing by.)* Are you still talking about me?
             (Laughs.) What did you decide? Will we have peace?

             Silence.

PAUL: OK, I'll leave you guys alone. *(Walks away.)*

STAN: I understand what you mean. Although I have no
             first-hand experience I am sure that an immigrant's
             life is never easy. Take care, or *"Salaam"*, as you say.

BASSEL: *(Slightly laughing.)* Bye.

Scene 6
Cairo September 1993

> *An open air restaurant on the Nile in a Cairo suburb,*
> *Um-Kalsoum—the topmost Arab diva of the*
> *twentieth century—is singing "lel sabr houdoud":*
> *"There are limits to patience", in the background.*

BASSEL: Seleem, did you see the look on that guy's face?

SELEEM: Which guy, Bassel? That guy over there?

BASSEL: No you idiot, Rabin, the Israeli Prime Minister.

SELEEM: He's here? *(Laughs.)*

BASSEL: Try and be serious for once, Seleem. Did you see him on the TV?

SELEEM: On TV and in the papers. He did look quite disgusted when Arafat extended his hand.

BASSEL: I analyzed the photo. Arafat did all the traveling. Rabin didn't even move. And as they shook hands he didn't even make the effort to smile.

SELEEM: Since you are so good in analysis, why don't you analyze our lives and tell me, Bassel, are we going to be perpetual bachelors or is there still some hope of getting married?

BASSEL: Do you think of nothing else? We'll get married when we get married. Don't worry about it.

SELEEM: Everyone we know got married except us. I'm 35. Kamel's son is 6 years old. When will I have a 6 years old son? When I am 60?

BASSEL: You know, Kamel told me that he has a perfect match for me. A relative of his wife. He wanted to introduce me to her.

SELEEM: And of course you are still opposed to this type of marriage. It doesn't suit your Western way of life. *(Laughs.)*

BASSEL: Here we go again.

SELEEM: OK, OK. But you did refuse.

BASSEL: Of course I did.

SELEEM: How come no one ever makes me such offers?

BASSEL: It can't happen that way. It has to be natural. Otherwise it is like Rabin's handshake. Forced on you.

SELEEM: Politics, politics. What is so strange about Rabin's attitude? They fetched Arafat from the memory of history to be their peace partner. They needed him to stop the *"Intifada."* We all know this. So "Play your role and don't come upstairs and shake my hand in front of everybody." They should have made it clear to him.

BASSEL: Unfortunately, your sarcasm reflects the sad reality. It is not a peace that can last. How much I wished that a new era would begin and that Egypt would prosper as it should.

SELEEM: And why is it not prospering already? We are in "peace" since the seventies.

BASSEL: I don't know. I just don't want to lose hope. It feels so bad that all the guys we know have university degrees and hold steady jobs yet no one can afford to even repaint his apartment.

SELEEM: We just don't have "corruption" skills. That's the problem. We don't know how to play the system.

BASSEL: Sad.

SELEEM: And I can't even get married.

BASSEL: *(With a sigh.)* Again...Tell you what, I'll guarantee you that before the Oslo agreement is implemented you will be married.

SELEEM: *(Fake laugh.)* Ha, ha, ha. You pretty well know that it will never be implemented. Let's try something else, how about before the pound reaches 10 for a dollar?...Is this too soon?

BASSEL: *(Sadly.)* I hope not.

SELEEM: Look, I need something now. Can't wait anymore. A piece of chocolate cake would be good. *(Laughs.)* They have great chocolate cake here... *(Calls out.)* Waiter!

Scene 7
Montreal, April 1995

TV on, the date—April 19, 1995—is mentioned. Oklahoma bombing mentioned...establish then under.

Door opens.

BASSEL: Hi, how was your day?

HÉLÈNE: Pas mal, how was yours?

BASSEL: Did you hear about Oklahoma City.

HÉLÈNE: Who hasn't? Did they say who did it?

BASSEL: *(Int.)* Here it comes. *(Ext.)* Analysts are analyzing and specialists are speculating.

HÉLÈNE: Who?

BASSEL: They don't know for sure.

HÉLÈNE: Who do they think it is?

BASSEL: The usual suspects!

HÉLÈNE: *(Frustrated.)* Why don't you want to say it, it is Muslims, isn't it?

BASSEL: *(On the defensive.)* They *(Stresses the word.)* speculate Arabs, Middle Easterners, Muslims. Most are speculating. No one knows.

HÉLÈNE: *(On the offensive.)* I knew it.

BASSEL: What did you know? How could you *(Stresses.)* know when no one knows anything yet?

HÉLÈNE: *(Fake support.)* I understand your position. But, dear, who could it be? It can be no one else. And please, don't take it personally. You are different, very different. *(Laughs politely.)* You just have to take one more step and rid yourself of all this once and for all. You are not one of them. You just have to accept it.

BASSEL: *(To himself but loud enough for HÉLÈNE to hear.)* Yes, I have to take one more step. *(Louder.)* Hélène, they don't know who did it. No one does. Don't you think that I too think it has to do with the "usual suspects"? I do, but if the North American values are what they are claimed to be then no one should be saying it until there is proof.

HÉLÈNE: What proof do you want?

BASSEL: Proof. Like legal proof. How can you have such double standards?

HÉLÈNE: *(Angry.)* Don't get your frustration of your own people out on me. I do *(Stresses.)* not have double standards.

BASSEL: Helene, I did not mean you. I meant society as a whole. Criminals and crime lords have the right to ridiculously lengthy trials at the taxpayer's expense, while millions can be condemned without even waiting till the dust, literally, settles; and, now that you say it, you are not acting any different. You already condemned without trial. You do suffer from the same double standards.

HÉLÈNE: I've had enough. For years I have been patient with you. I thought you were progressing. Coming along. But I can see that it was all fake. And one day I loved you!

BASSEL: *(Stresses the past tense.)* Loved. That's really nice.

HÉLÈNE: Bassel, look, it's not working out.

BASSEL: And why is that? I'm really interested to know your reasoning.

HÉLÈNE: I don't want to hurt you.

BASSEL: You already did. For years I've been trying to work out things between us. I was willing to keep trying, but maybe I was wrong.

HÉLÈNE: You are wrong. We'll never see eye-to-eye. You should have found yourself a nice Muslim woman who thinks the same way you do from the beginning. I...I thought you would become a civilized person...

BASSEL: That's enough Hélène. Don't say one more word, please. I don't want either of us to say anything we'll regret later. It's over. Let it be over in a respectable way.

HÉLÈNE: I'll be out of here in a couple of days. Bonne nuit.

Door slams, not too loud.

Scene 8
A Coffee Shop in Cairo, April 1995

Eastern music in the background, Arabic words, etc. continues throughout the scene.

BASSEL: And he wasn't even Arab, Muslim or in any way related. The exact opposite actually.

SELEEM: Was he supposed to be? Maybe he didn't know it was not the part to be played by an American. What was his name, Bassel?

BASSEL: *(Badly pronounced.)* McVeigh, Timothy McVeigh.

SELEEM: *"Aaaah."* Nice name.

BASSEL: You are—again—taking this too lightly.

SELEEM: What difference does it make? How does it affect us?

BASSEL: Can't you see that it means a lot. Day after day new incidents occur that prove that the West looks at us the wrong way. They don't—deep inside—accept the one world vision they superficially advocate.

SELEEM: It's only dreamers like you who believed that. Although you never did cross the straight of Gibraltar physically, you did cross it mentally and emotionally. Maybe there are dreamers like you over there too. Who knows? The world is full of strange things. (Laughs.)

BASSEL: One day I did believe in that. I still do, to a certain extent, but in a more realistic way now.

SELEEM: Hey, you seem to be crossing back to us, (Laughs.) welcome home.

BASSEL: Anyway, I have to go.

SELEEM: Why? It's still early. Are you called in by the "high authority"?

BASSEL: You know Laila is pregnant and doesn't go out much. I have to be home more.

SELEEM: What month is she in?

BASSEL: Sixth. As if you understand anything about such things.

SELEEM: Just wanted to know. Maybe one day I'll be in the same boat. Remember when you were saying you'd never get married.

BASSEL: I didn't say that.

SELEEM: Right, right…you just said it has to happen the right way. And then zap, without introductions. What happened there? Don't misunderstand me, Laila is great and all, but what happened to "It has to happen the right way. No one will find me a wife." And all that.

BASSEL: They don't have to be contradictory. It is true that Laila was introduced to me with the purpose of marriage but I found her a suitable person that I can honestly say I fell in love with.

SELEEM: *Habeebee*, you got married when you brought your expectations down a notch or two, and I again don't mean that Laila is bad in any way, so don't get me in trouble. As for me, I will get married when women bring their expectations down. Down quite a few notches. *(Laughs.)*

BASSEL: We're not young anymore. Now that I am expecting a son, I wish I could have had him when I was 30.

SELEEM: You were about to. Then came your emigration plan that turned your life upside down. She was ready. Remember her? I am sure she would have bought the wedding dress the next day. But you are the one who said I am off to Canada... I hear she got married right after you two broke up.

BASSEL: *(Stresses.)* "She" now is a mother of three. All that seems to have happened in another lifetime. We walk the steps which we have to walk. Nothing happens before, or after, its time. *(Assertive.)* Got to go.

SELEEM: I guess now was the time. *(Laughs.)* "Yalla," I'll go too. Say Salaam to Laila. Tell her to find me a wife. Be of some use to your friend.

Scene 9
Montreal, September 1997

>   *Hiking trail on Mont Royal, People, dogs, kids,*
> *throughout the scene.*

BASSEL: *"Salaam"* Salwa.

SALWA: *(Has an accent—French influence.) "Salaam Alaikum"* Bassel, sorry I am late. How are you?

BASSEL: OK, *"al-hamd-u le-Lah."* How are you and how is school?

SALWA: School work is not going well. I am late in my thesis and, if I want to finish anytime soon, should spend all my time at the university.

BASSEL: Is your professor still being a pain.

SALWA: *(Laughs.)* Nothing like my professors in France, at least. With all the difficulties I sometimes face here, it is still pretty good. A friend of mine in Paris used to say, "The city of light is so dark for Algerians, especially practicing Muslims".

BASSEL: Imagine if you were wearing a veil!

SALWA: You know I still am thinking of doing that, and if I decide to, it is not how some people treat me that will stop me. Bad treatment never stopped anyone, look around you. It maybe the opposite, actually.

BASSEL: Despite the fact that we don't agree about the veil and how religiously significant it is, I know that a woman's veil is not the problem. The problem is the veil that covers the minds of those who can't accept it.

            Silence. Background sounds more obvious.

SALWA: It's a sad day today.

BASSEL: Why, what happened?

SALWA: What do you mean what happened? Everyone's sad about Diana's death.

BASSEL: I guess I have no feelings. *(Laughs politely.)*

SALWA: Men will never feel these things the same way

women do. The poor woman had a difficult life, and when things started to lighten up, she dies. And only God knows how.

BASSEL: Conspiracies. Conspiracy theories are as popular here as they are in our countries. *(Laughs. More serious.)* Still, even the most objective mind can't ignore that many would be uncomfortable if the King of England, and Canada, had an Egyptian stepfather.

Silence, background noises heard, and birds.

BASSEL: *(Hesitant.)* Salwa...I've been thinking.

SALWA: *(Serious.)* About what?

BASSEL: Us.

SALWA: So have I.

BASSEL: Every time I tell you about a party, or ask you to join me for dinner with some friends, you refuse.

SALWA: It is always in a bar, or somewhere where alcohol is served. I am never comfortable in those places. You know that. I am not like your previous *(Stresses.)* friends.

BASSEL: I know you are not. And I appreciate you for what you are. I would love to live a more disciplined life myself, pray five times a day, like you do, but I can't. I am myself and if I change it will have to be gradual.

SALWA: But I never asked you to. I am only asking you not to try to change me.

BASSEL: But meanwhile life has to go on. And you don't want to live in the real world. We cannot create our own universe and live in it. I cannot live isolated from the world.

SALWA: I was clear from the beginning. We discussed all this before.

BASSEL: I agreed that we will not be intimate before
             marriage. I agreed that we will define ourselves as
             Muslims …

SALWA: *(Interrupts.)* It's not a theoretical definition, Bassel.

BASSEL: I know, I know, that's why I am talking about it
             now.

SALWA: I will make it easier for you. It is not going to work
             out. I admire you, but we are too far apart and it is…

BASSEL: I am sorry.

SALWA: Don't be. You may be under a different impression,
             but I have never told my parents about us, as I once
             said I would. Every time I am about to tell them on
             the phone or write to them about it I feel that it is
             better not to, because I, myself, am far from being
             convinced that it will work out between us.

BASSEL: Thanks for understanding.

SALWA: Thank you for understanding my position too. I'd
             better go now.

BASSEL: Would you like to go for dinner, one last time?

SALWA: I'd better go back to school and try to get some work
             done. *"Salaam"* Bassel. Take care of yourself.

BASSEL: You too, Salwa. All the best.

             BASSEL's footsteps, background noises.

Scene 10
Cairo, Bassel's Apartment: September 1997

             *A two-year-old babbling, Arabic TV or radio
             newscast fades out after a few minutes.*

             Phone rings.

BASSEL: *(Loud.)* Laila, I'll send you Rami. I need to get the
             phone.

LAILA:	My hands are dirty, Bassel. I'll be with you in a second.
BASSEL:	*Allo.*
	Silence…
	Of course I heard. *(Pause.)* Of course…
LAILA:	Here, come here Rami.
RAMI:	Baba. Baba.
BASSEL:	It is suspicious but… *(Pause.)*
LAILA:	Who's that?
BASSEL:	*(To the party on the phone.)* Just a second. *(To LAILA.)* Kamel. *(Back to the phone.)* Yes Kamel *(Pause.)* No *(Pause.)* OK, we'll talk soon. Salaam.
LAILA:	What was that about? What's suspicious?
BASSEL:	What do you think? What's the talk of the town, the country, the world? Diana's death of course.
LAILA:	It is not suspicious, it is certain that they killed her, and him, and the child.
BASSEL:	What child?
LAILA:	The child she was carrying. The Muslim brother of the King of England.
BASSEL:	*"Ahlan,"* Madam Shakespeare. And there was a child too!?
LAILA:	Spare me your sarcasm, Bassel. Whether she was pregnant or not, there was a man who was very close to become stepfather to the future king of England. And that man was a Muslim. Does it not make sense that many people would not want that to happen?
BASSEL:	Let's say there were. Does that make it a fact? Does this prove murder?

LAILA: What make was the car? Isn't Mercedes one of the safest cars in the world? Look at the photos. How could a normal accident do that to the car? People of that stature don't die in car accidents.

BASSEL: Actually they do. Grace Kelly of Monaco, for example.

LAILA: That's beside the point; you'd do anything to prove the West innocent.

BASSEL: The West!?

LAILA: Yes, the West. That culture you always wanted to be a part of.

BASSEL: Laila, please. You know I could have, and I never did. Why this again?

LAILA: Poor Diana was killed and the whole world knows it. Al-Fayed, his father, says the same thing.

BASSEL: Al-Fayed is a business man. The rules of his game are very different. And this Muslim stepfather thing, what is Muslim to you people? Is Muslim a birthright or is it a way of life? Was this Dodi character a "Muslim"?

LAILA: *(Serious and raising her voice a little.)* Bassel, this is something between him and his Lord. Not for you to judge.

BASSEL: OK, OK, you're right.

LAILA: And second, even if we forget Muslim. He is Arab. He is an intruder into their world. He has a place, and his place is "downstairs." Muslim or not he will never be accepted in their world.

BASSEL: Contrary to what you said about me, and my admiration for the West, I do agree to a certain extent. The whole Fayed family, rich and powerful as they may be, are not able to obtain British citizenship till today.

LAILA: See, now you took off the Westerner's hat you were wearing and became normal.

BASSEL: And for that I have to accept that it was murder?

            Phone rings.

            (Answers phone.) "Allo" (Pause.)

            Hello Seleem. How are you?

            Baby cries.

LAILA: *(To baby.) "Bass, bass."*

            Dinner will be ready in a few minutes.

BASSEL: *(To SELEEM.)* No, no, *(Sarcastically.)* of course it was a murder. No, no doubt.

Scene 11
Montreal, September 2001

            Typing on the keyboard, sipping coffee, phone rings.

BASSEL: Hello.

SARA: *(On the phone.)* Bassel!

BASSEL: *(Surprised.)* Sara?! Is everything OK? Are you feeling any pain?

SARA: I'm fine, I'm fine.

BASSEL: Thank God. What's up then? *(Pause.)* Why aren't you saying anything? I left you less than an hour ago and all was fine.

SARA: Didn't you hear about the planes in New York?

BASSEL: What planes in New York?

SARA: Two planes hit the two towers of the World Trade Center in New York. Some say it is an attack.

BASSEL: Are you sure? I'll check the net. Talk to you soon. You take care of yourself and don't exhaust yourself. Bye. *(Hangs the phone.)*

           Footsteps.

STAN: *(Moving on.)* Both World Trade Center towers were hit. Did you know?

BASSEL: Sara just called me. I was focused on finishing this report since I came in. I didn't even read my email yet.

STAN: No accident for sure. Is there a TV somewhere?

BASSEL: Not on this floor. There's one upstairs, in Marketing.

BASSEL: *(Loud to someone far.)* Jim. *(To STAN.)* This kid is on the net all day—I always catch him browsing. Let him be useful for a change. *(To JIM who is now close.)* What did you hear?

JIM: The world is a mess, man.

BASSEL: Do you think it's an accident?

JIM: I don't know, and I don't care.

STAN: It's really something. How could terrorists get hold of three planes at the same time?

BASSEL: Three? What three?

STAN: There's one that hit the Pentagon.

BASSEL: Oh my God!

STAN: I guess it's clear now. It's an attack on America.

BASSEL: That's bad.

           Footsteps. JIM moves off.

STAN: Sure, and frightening.

BASSEL: And it's surely going to be "blame the usual suspects". Remember Oklahoma.

STAN: This time there is no doubt who did it.

BASSEL: What do you mean?

STAN: *(Avoids answering, regrets his previous statement.)* I'll go upstairs to see what they are saying on TV. *(Moves off.)*

JIM: *(Moves on.)* Who needs TV? The net is a million times better than TV. There they say it all.

BASSEL: Analysts are on TV right away. I bet you they have that guy, Emerson—spreading his wisdom as he did in 1995—on CNN. So many lives were wasted. So many will still be wasted because we don't learn. *(More to himself.)* Obviously we don't learn if they are already claiming they know who did it.

JIM: I didn't say anything, boss. I'll get back to work.

         Phone rings.

BASSEL: Hello.

SARA: *(On the phone.)* Do you know what they are saying on TV?

BASSEL: I know what they must be saying. I don't need to hear the radio or watch TV. You take it easy. You know that you are having a difficult pregnancy and we don't want anything bad to happen.

SARA: I will. But I am worried about my father.

BASSEL: Your father shouldn't have a problem. He's travelling with a Canadian passport.

SARA: But they'll know. His passport says he's born in Syria. They'll know he is an Arab. And he's flying through the States on his way back. Anything can happen to him.

BASSEL: I don't think matters will reach that stage. I'll try to get in touch with him soon and let you know. You take care of yourself and take it easy.

SARA: You take it easy too. Don't get into arguments.

BASSEL: Will try to stay calm. Please don't give birth today. *(Laughs.)* We don't want her to be linked to this dark day. *Salaam.*

BASSEL: *(Int.)* For the first time since I came here I am afraid. Personally afraid. Am I afraid for myself or for the girl that I am bringing to this world during these difficult times? Is she going to be born on the wrong side of the world?

STAN: *(Moving on.)* Bassel, one of the World Trade Center towers just collapsed.

BASSEL: So many lives wasted. *(Pause.)* So many.

Scene 12
Egypt, A Mediterranean Resort: September 2001

Quiet beach, sound of waves, a toddler playing in the sand, Eastern music.

BASSEL: Come, Rami. Let's go home.

RAMI: *(Makes objecting noises—six year old refusal—firm.)* No.

SELEEM: *(Hurrying—out of breath—moving on.)* Bassel. *(Closer.)* Bassel, where are you man? Sitting here relaxing while the world is upside down?

BASSEL: What's wrong Seleem? Rami is happy here. Let him enjoy some peace. What's going on anyway?

SELEEM: America is being attacked.

BASSEL: What do you mean? Sit. Sit and catch your breath.

SELEEM: *(Still short of breath.)* It is not a joke. The World Trade Center towers in New York are falling. Two planes crashed in them. A terrorist attack.

BASSEL: May God have mercy on the world. What planes? Tell me the details.

SELEEM: That's all we know. Two civilian planes—obviously hijacked —hit the two towers and one of them fell.

BASSEL: That's horrible.

SELEEM: Yeah, but it had to happen. Uncle Sam has been killing people all around the world for decades. Sooner or later he had to reap the fruit of his actions.

BASSEL: What time did that happen?

SELEEM: Within the past two hours. Nine in the morning, their time.

BASSEL: Meaning employees were at work. So many must have died. That's so bad.

SELEEM: How many died in Vietnam? How many kids died in Iraq in the last ten years because of the sanctions? Wake up man!

BASSEL: No, Seleem. You wake up! Two wrongs don't make a right. You wake up. What are the women saying?

SELEEM: My wife is crying. Laila says they got what they deserve.

BASSEL: Nobody deserves that. We have to start thinking with our heads not our emotions. This won't make things better for the Palestinians. The sanctions on Iraq won't end. Now that I think about it, it's going to be the exact opposite. It's just going to get worse.

SELEEM: Things were already getting worse by the day. America had to understand that it is not invincible.

BASSEL: No one is invincible. Empires come and empires go.

SELEEM: It's a lesson. You can't equate those who react to
                 years of aggression with the aggressor, can you?

BASSEL: *(Not listening.)* Did they say who did it?

SELEEM: That's another issue. I am sure they would say some
                 extremist Muslim group. My problem is that I don't
                 think those guys have the skill or the organization to
                 perform such an operation.

BASSEL: Is this another conspiracy theory of yours?

SELEEM: No, I didn't formulate one yet. *(Laughs.)*

BASSEL: You're right not to. This whole issue demands that
                 we reflect calmly. And I was thinking—just before
                 you came—that it was a very calm day. The calm
                 that precedes the storm, it seems to have been.

RAMI: *(Cries.)*

BASSEL: It seems Rami's day is also turning around.

SELEEM: Or he may just have gotten some sand in his eye.
                 Let's go back to the cabin; his mother will take care
                 of him.

BASSEL: *(Moving, low voice, nearly whispering.)* And who will
                 take care of the rest of us in this madness?

Scene 13
Downtown Montreal, Bassel on a walk during his
lunch break: 12:15 EDT 2002/09/11

                 Footsteps, street noises, car horns.

BASSEL: *(Int.)* I thought the first anniversary of 9-11 was
                 going to be worse than this. Half the day is over and
                 it wasn't bad. No silly remarks. No unfounded
                 allegations.

GIRL: *(To someone a few steps ahead of BASSEL.)* A flower for
                 the victims?

BASSEL: *(Int.)* That's nice. Should I take one? That should help change some stereotype. *(Pause.)* Why am I not comfortable about this?

GIRL: *(Int.)* Do I give that guy who looks Arab a flower? Would he want one?

BASSEL: *(Int.)* She's avoiding eye contact. I'd better just walk by.

GIRL: *(Int.)* He's avoiding me. I'll ignore him.

BASSEL: *(Int.)* I'll avoid her.

               Footsteps.

BASSEL: *(Int.)* Strange that now more than ever I am wondering if I took the right decision immigrating to Canada. I would have surely been happier if I would have stayed in Egypt. *(Pause, then very assertively.)* Surely.

Scene 14
Cairo, A Shop, 11 September 2002

               Car horns, pedestrians and merchants.

BASSEL: Excuse me, how much is that?

MERCHANT: Thirty-five.

BASSEL: *(Int.)* Too expensive. *(To LAILA.)* How come everything has become so expensive?

LAILA: It's not nice anyway. I'll go see that one over there. Come Rami.

BASSEL: *(Int.)* That's a view of New York City when the World Trade Center towers were still standing. Difficult to imagine it was exactly a year ago today.

               Shoppers' sounds in Arabic in the background.

BASSEL: *(Int.)* Now that's a nice picture. It will probably cost a fortune. Looks like a dreamland. A lovely green, green mountain with a lit cross on top. I can't read the text. *(Tries to get closer—to another customer.)* Excuse me.

Shoppers' sounds in Arabic in the background.

BASSEL: The Mont-Royal. Montreal, Quebec. *(Louder.)* Oh my God! Can't even imagine how I would have been doing if I would have been living there now. Had to be better than being here. I would probably be totally Canadian by now. *(Sarcastically.)* Mister Bassel. Good morning. *(Faking French accent.)* Bonjour.

BASSEL: Surely I would have been happier if I would have gone there. *(Pause.)* Surely.

The End.

Wanderers

Marco Micone

translated from the French
by Sheila Fischman

Marco Micone

Marco Micone was born in Southern Italy in 1945 and emigrated to Canada with his family in 1958. He grew up in Montreal and earned French degrees at Loyola and McGill. At the latter he wrote an MA thesis on the theatre of Marcel Dubé. His first play, *Gens du silence* was staged in 1980 at Le Théatre de l'Ouverture and was published in 1982. The English version, *Voiceless People*, premiered in Vancouver in 1986. As the first French-language play to examine the immigrant experience in Québec it achieved critical and popular success with repeated productions. Later plays include *Addolorata* (1994) *Déjà l'agonie* (1988). Micone's plays explore Québec politics and the place of immigrants in a separatist society, questions that he also engages in his essays *Le Figuier enchanté* (1992).

About the Play

Wanderers is set is Quebec in the 1970s and Italy a decade and a half later. Luigi is a Canadian of Italian heritage; he was married to a Québécois woman and while married they had a son, Nino—now a teenager. Luigi has taken Nino back to his parents' ancestral village in Southern Italy, the son's first visit. Nino's grandparents had returned there from Montreal, because the grandfather wanted to live where his memories were. But the memories aren't all good—not by a long shot—and the visit of the grandson and his questioning stirs things up. But the grandson also finds his view of the world changing—what was a boring journey becomes an act of finding his own roots in the world.

Cast

FRANCO: .... Gerry Mendicino

MARIA: .... Angela Fusco

LUIGI: .... Angelo Celeste

DANIELLE: .... Patricia Marceau

NINO: .... Adamo Ruggiero

Characters

FRANCO: .... the grandfather

MARIA: .... the grandmother

LUIGI: .... the son

DANIELLE: .... Luigi's ex-wife

NINO: .... son of Luigi and Danielle, 15

Production Credits

Producer/Director: .... Damiano Pietropaolo

Associate Producer: .... Colleen Wooods

Original Music: .... Claudio Vena

Casting: .... Linda Grearson

Recording Engineer: .... Greg De Clute

Sound Effects: .... Matt Wilcott

Scene 1

> *Late 1980s. Summer night in a village in southern Italy. NINO and LUIGI.*
>
> *Music: Theme, establish then under...*
>
> *Summer night insects, dogs in the distance, bells tolling the time*
>
> *Two sets of steps walking on cobblestones...*

LUIGI: *(Presses an imaginary windowpane with his hand.)* In the winter, when you were little, we'd put our hands on the window and the frost would melt. You would draw a hill with your finger...and I'd talk to you about my childhood.

NINO: Where is home, Papa?

LUIGI: Look, just there, on the right—that was my uncle's house.

NINO: It hasn't got any doors or windows!

LUIGI: My uncle has been in Argentina for thirty years... Why would he need doors and windows here?

NINO: Where did you used to live, Papa? Where is it? Where?

LUIGI: Over there, in back of the church.

NINO: What a weird thing to do, arrive here at night! We can't see a thing.

LUIGI: It's as if everything has stopped...as if nothing exists except you and me.

NINO: I smell something burning.

LUIGI: That's from stubble burning in the valley.

NINO: There's black dust over everything...I've got it...on my hands...my shirt. When do we get there?... Where is home, Papa?

            Gurgling stream in the distance.

LUIGI: Over there, near the light that's flickering in the wind.

NINO: Another house with no door or windows.

LUIGI: That's normal...it's the old part of the village. Listen, listen...

NINO: I can't hear anything... I can't hear a thing ...

LUIGI: The stream...

NINO: You can hear a stream?

LUIGI: It runs right next to our place...I'll take you there tomorrow.

            Music: Fades up and bridges to next scene and resolves...

Scene 2

            MARIO, FRANCO, LUIGI and DANIELLE.

            Montreal, early 1970s. MARIA and FRANCO in the kitchen. LUIGI arrives with DANIELLE.

            MARIA is cooking in the kitchen.

            Door opens.

MARIA: *(Off.)* Is that you, Luigi?

            Door closes.

FRANCO: *(To his son.)* What are you doing here? Begging for money again? Can't even pay your rent... *(Not hostile, more out of habit.)*

Door closes.

FRANCO: You lazy good-for-nothing...

DANIELLE: Bon jour...

MARIA: *(Still off.)* Who's that with you?

LUIGI: I told you on the phone...it's Danielle.

MARIA: *(Approaching.)* Danielle who?

DANIELLE: Danielle Cormier.

MARIA: Another French-Canadian!

LUIGI: She has an Italian uncle.

DANIELLE: He comes from Firenze.

FRANCO: He's a liar. Nobody leaves Firenze to come here.

DANIELLE: His village isn't far from Florence...he used to go there on foot ...

MARIA: Did you have supper?

LUIGI: *(Smiles.)* Of course, Mamma.

DANIELLE: I can't wait to taste your cooking. I'm sure it's a hundred times better than Luigi's!

MARIA: Tell her to learn Italian...*our* Italian. The tenant's leaving in two months... That gives you time to get married...

LUIGI: We live...

FRANCO: *(Interrupts LUIGI.)* She'll leave him before...just like the others, she'll leave him...

LUIGI: *(Answering his mother.)* We're already living together.

MARIA: Living together? Without being married?

LUIGI: It's no worse than being married and not living together...

MARIA and
FRANCO: We...

MARIA: ...it was the only thing we could do.

FRANCO: So that's why you left home...to do whatever you
               want... *(Heads for the door.)*

LUIGI: Papa! Don't leave now...listen...you don't
               understand...for us, marriage isn't important,
               we...here, sit down...talk to me...

MARIA: ...to shame us...

               Door opens ....

LUIGI: Mamma! Why are you running away from me?...
               I've got so many things to tell you ...

               ...And closes... FRANCO and MARIA exit.

               *Music: Abandonment theme...continues under next
               scene...*

               I didn't see him till I was thirteen, Danielle.
               Belgium, Switzerland, Venezuela, always on his
               own...and then we all came here...two
               strangers...we're two strangers...

DANIELLE: I'd never have imagined...your parents...it's as if
               they just got here yesterday.

               Theme is featured for ten seconds or so, then under...

Scene 3

               Italy, July, late 1980s. LUIGI and NINO. Daytime.

               Mediterranean cicadas, cats in the distance.

               Footsteps on cobblestones...

NINO: *(Enthusiastic.)* I hear a baby crying...

LUIGI: There are two...there's two babies crying, Nino...

What did I tell you? Everyone's in bed...tomorrow morning we'll be wakened by the town crier and I'll go out and buy figs and Muscat...

We hear cats squalling.

NINO: *(NINO very disappointed.)* It was cats, Papa...just cats.

A memory of bells, an echo of the feast...

LUIGI: Here's the main square. On feast days people come from all over...there, in the middle, is the orchestra, and all around, there are games for the children...we sing and dance and eat till morning.

Thunder in the far distance...approaching as the scene ends...

NINO: Where are the flowers? You told me there'd be flowers on all the balconies.

LUIGI: There's going to be a storm tonight... You can't leave flowers outside...

NINO: It's not true...there's nobody in the village at all.

LUIGI: You're here...and I am...nobody's missing...

NINO: *(Interrupts him.)* You should have brought me when there were still people living in the village...I would have made friends...Why did you all go away?

Music: Abandonment theme fades up and is featured...then fades under...and resolves.

Scene 4

Montreal, early 1970s. FRANCO and MARIA finish packing two suitcases.

Suitcases being packed and handled...light traffic outside.

LUIGI: You've packed your bags...are you going somewhere?

                Suitcases being shut, first one then another.

FRANCO: There's nothing for us here.

MARIA: The house in the village is falling apart... We have to fix it...

FRANCO: *(This line overlaps part of the previous one.)* ...we're going home...I'm not interested in anything that goes on here...it doesn't concern me... All I've done here is work... Here, I'm nobody... I want to live the rest of my life in a place with memories...

                FRANCO walks off with suitcase, door opens...

                ...a place where everything I see is also inside me...

                And closes...

LUIGI: You hear that, Mamma? He'll never come back here. He'll force you to stay in the village... You've always hated that village...You've always said it was no place for women... Why are you leaving?... Let him go... He'll be better off on his own... He's always preferred to be alone... Don't go, Mamma... You know this is a better place for you...What will you do in a heap of stones?... Stay... I'll come and see you every day... Let him go by himself...

MARIA: I'll never do that to him.

                Music: The journey back...establish under...

                I'll...we'll come back...

LUIGI: He's always lied to you... Remember Argentina... He was supposed to stay there for six months... How many years did we wait for him?... How many years?...

                Music: Feature as bridge to next scene then under...

Scene 5

Italy, July night, late 1980s. NINO and LUIGI.

Nightime village ambience as per Scene 1...

Low thunder in the distance.

Steps on cobblestones.

LUIGI: Right here, outside Angela's house, was where we built the fire for Saint Anthony... She'd be there on her balcony and I'd sit here and watch her every night for two weeks.

NINO: *(Upset at what his father has just said.)* Did you ever come here with Mamma?

LUIGI: Just once...we left the next day. What are you doing? Why did you stop?

NINO: It's too dark.

LUIGI: Let's walk faster... There's more light on the street over there...

            Steps speed up...

NINO: There were still people here and you only stayed for one day?

LUIGI: When we arrived it was just like this...very late at night...everybody was in bed...we'd left the car near the fountain so we wouldn't make any noise...and we walked to that door... That's where I was born... Your mother was beside me, like you are now... I ducked my head and went inside... I climbed the stairs in the dark, opened the door and turned on a light. There was one yellowish light bulb hanging from the ceiling that gave me just enough light to see the fly specks all over the twisted electrical cord. Nothing had changed: the wobbly table, the four straw-bottomed chairs, the bread box by the fireplace...and in the valley, the

burning stubble. Everything was like it had been
before. Your mother was on the balcony, watching
fire move up the hill in waves, and saying over and
over: *"It's so beautiful...so beautiful!"*

Music: "It's so beautiful"...under.

It took me back to the dark winter nights, and the
stale bread and the water that froze in its pitcher on
the night table. I heard your mother say again: *It's so
beautiful.* It was getting late, I could hardly stand up,
so I sat down under the flickering light and I saw my
grandmother again, huddled by the fireplace and
poking at the embers that were nearly dead, my
sister embroidering her boredom onto her endless
trousseau, and myself with my history book,
learning to hate the Austrians, and then running off
to serve mass. Just then your mother came in and
when she saw how glum I looked, she could barely
stammer: *It's so... (Brief pause.)* We left the next day
without getting a wink of sleep... *(Beat.)* I hear my
mother's voice.

NINO: If you decide to leave tomorrow, Papa, it's fine with
me.

Low thunder in distance.

Music: Bridge to next scene...

Scene 6

*Montreal, early 1970s. DANIELLE and LUIGI
looking at their agendas.*

Light traffic outside.

*French radio in background with items about the
language issues....*

DANIELLE: Tomorrow night I've got a meeting with the party's
wage-equity committee.

LUIGI: Tomorrow night? I've got a meeting of the committee to support political refugees.

DANIELLE: Monday night, our committee's executive meeting.

LUIGI: Founding meeting of an alternative newspaper.

DANIELLE: Tuesday night we're both at a meeting to translate the Party program into Italian.

LUIGI: I've decided not to go.

DANIELLE: You promised.

LUIGI: I can't translate a program I don't totally agree with. I'll send somebody...

DANIELLE: Wednesday, there's the demonstration in support of the French language.

LUIGI: I'm down for two meetings at the same time.

DANIELLE: Thursday I deliver a speech to all the Party delegates.

LUIGI: Thursday? But Thursday's our anniversary...our first anniversary...I've invited some of our friends... I thought ...

DANIELLE: I really can't...it's very important to me...

LUIGI: Then we'll celebrate on Friday.

DANIELLE: You've forgotten, we're both at the same meeting... *(Silence, then, enthusiastic.)* Wasn't that a fantastic demonstration last night! Ten thousand people at least.

LUIGI: I've never seen so many immigrants.

DANIELLE: Or so many women. There's something happening that we don't understand yet...something very important... You could sense it last night, it was palpable...we can't waste any more time...we saw last night...everyone's ready for a change...a real change…everything's going to be different. You could see it in people's eyes…we've been waiting for so long… *(Looks at her watch.)* Seven o'clock already? My meeting starts in fifteen minutes. I have to run.

LUIGI: I wanted to talk to you about our trip in February…our holidays…

DANIELLE: Sure, good idea… We should go to South America.

LUIGI: South America? I refuse to put money into a military regime.

DANIELLE: A friend of mine went to the Dominican Republic. She said it was terrific.

LUIGI: Can you see yourself in a restaurant while little kids in rags stare at you wide-eyed with their noses pressed to the window?

DANIELLE: Let's go back to Cuba then!

LUIGI: Again?

Scene 7

July night, late 1980s, LUIGI and NINO in the village with FRANCO and MARIA.

Nightime village ambience, the church clock has been tolling the time…

Music: "Reunion" joins with sound effects to create a magical, happy atmosphere…

LUIGI: You've been back in the village for fifteen years, Mamma… You were supposed to be staying for two months…I told you he wouldn't leave here again.

MARIA: Your father and I have been happy here.

LUIGI: You would have come to Montreal… *(Talking about*

his father.) He's the one who wouldn't let you leave... He's the one who stopped you...

MARIA: What about you, why didn't you come till now?

Music: Picks up on mother's sense of loss and longing and resolves under...

LUIGI: I couldn't...I couldn't leave my work...

FRANCO: (*Mocking.*) Couldn't leave your work... You call that work, what you do? (*Out of habit.*) You lazy good-for-nothing...

NINO: Let's go, Papa.

LUIGI: No matter what you think, I've always worked...

FRANCO: A waste of time... What do you get out of it?

LUIGI: Nothing...nothing that matters to you anyway.

FRANCO: All those years of school for nothing! You do a job any idiot could do.

NINO: Why are you staying, Papa?

LUIGI: I like what I do and I'll do it all my life... I deal with immigrants...immigrants like you, who need someone who understands them and helps them and stands up for them...people like you and Mamma... If you'd taken any interest in me...if you'd taken an interest in my work, you would have realized that the work I do is necessary... important...maybe you'd have been proud of me... You wouldn't have run away from me... You wouldn't have come here and cut yourself off from the world...

FRANCO: I'm here because this is home.

MARIA: It's your home too, Luigi.

Music: Homelessness...longing...lost childhood...

Establish under then into next scene…

LUIGI: I have no idea where home is… But I do know that it's not just one place and that there's always something missing, no matter where I am…it's only when I go somewhere else that I feel as if where I was before was home.

FRANCO: If you'd had a house of your own…and a family…a real family…

LUIGI: *(LUIGI turns towards NINO.)* This heat is terrible! I'm parched. Let's go, Nino, let's go to the fountain. *(They exit.)*

MARIA: His family is us…and Nino… We can't go on living so far apart …

FRANCO: You and me, we'll always be together.

Scene 8

Italy, late 1980s. LUIGI and NINO at the fountain.

Nightime village ambience.

Trickle of dripping water from the fountain.

Music continues under…

NINO: The fountain's dried up, Papa.

LUIGI: *(Int.: Carried away by his memories, LUIGI doesn't hear him.)* Angela used to come to the fountain at the same time every day… She would fill her jug with water and her mother would set it on her head like a crown… She wore red sandals and a dress that rippled with every step she took… She was blonde…the only blonde in the village… The day when the jug spilled and her dress stuck to her skin, I prayed to all the saints in heaven for her to stand there forever like a caryatid… The same red sandals…the same blonde hair…the same dress, sticking to her skin...it was summer, we were at a demonstration...there were thousands of people...a storm had just burst... I took shelter under a tree...someone stepped back to make room for me...it was your mother, soaking wet from head to toe...

NINO: The fountain's dried up.

LUIGI: The water will come back next time it rains.

NINO: It won't make any difference, the women won't come back.

LUIGI: This is where the bus used to stop... It always stopped here...once a month, to take us away... Just the men at first ...

NINO: "...four or five at a time...then whole families. The day before I left, I'd gone to the countryside to hide under a straw hut... I'd brought bread and cheese to last for a few days... Two hours later I went to a farewell supper at my uncle's." I know all your stories by heart...you've told them a hundred times... You should have come by yourself, papa.

LUIGI: I wanted you to see with my eyes...to see the main square teeming with people, the little kids running all over the village and the fountain besieged by the women...like when you were little and in the winter, you'd draw a hill on the frost-covered windowpane while I told you about my childhood.

            Music is featured for a while then resolves...as bridge to next scene...

Scene 9

            Montreal, early 1970s. LUIGI and DANIELLE in their Montreal apartment. DANIELLE is pregnant.

            Light traffic outside...

LUIGI: This is the first time in three months, sweetheart, that you haven't got a meeting or a demonstration. *(Affectionate.)* Let me cuddle your belly and listen to the baby's heart.

DANIELLE: *(Ignores his request.)* You've hung a picture on this wall?

LUIGI: Me? Would I hang that picture of a toothless old geezer in a checked shirt and a ceinture fléchée... sitting in his rocking chair in front of a catalogne curtain?

DANIELLE: It's hideous.

LUIGI: It's a gift from your father.

DANIELLE: We have to get rid of it.

LUIGI: *(Mocking.)* Mademoiselle Cormier must have forgotten that every picture covers a hole or a crack in the wall. Mademoiselle has left her palace in Laval-sur-le-Lac, surrounded by weeping willows and magnolia trees. Now she's in a Mile End apartment, over a Chinese convenience store, in between a Greek souvlaki joint and a Portuguese fish store.

DANIELLE: Let's go out, I don't feel like staying inside all evening.

LUIGI: You haven't got a meeting or a demonstration tonight so I'd like to take you on a guided tour of our apartment. Here in front of us, you've got the kitchen and the worm-eaten table where the two of us, alone together, enjoyed a succulent supper of rice and lentils precisely fifty-six days ago. On your right, the windowless bed-chamber and on its floor, the tired old mattress which provides unassailable proof of your sincere and oh-so-moving conversion to poverty. And finally, here on your left, this rickety sofa, in classic Sally Ann style, mourns the loss of one of its cushions—torn to shreds by some cross-cultural rodents from our cosmopolitan sewers. Welcome to your salon, my love! *(Brief pause.)* You're right, let's go out, let's get the hell out of here! Such a beautiful evening! Perfect night for a demonstration...just the two of us... Why not go to the place where we met—outside the American consulate or, if you prefer, outside the Stock Exchange... Unless you'd rather that each of us goes to his own demonstration: you against English schools, me *(Provocatively.)* against Bill 101.

DANIELLE: *(Wounded.)* You'd do that? You'd really do that?

LUIGI: *(Briefly affectionate.)* Let me listen to the baby's heart.

DANIELLE: We have to move...we have to move to another part of town... I don't want my baby to be born in this slum.

LUIGI: *(Ironic.)* You're right, a year in this cesspool is more than enough...let's stop appropriating what doesn't belong to us...let's give poverty back to the poor...

DANIELLE: I can't stand that disgusting smell from the souvlaki joints, I'm sick of those immigrants in heat whistling at me on the street, I'm sick of buying fish from a Portuguese, fruit from an Italian, flowers from a Chinaman, I'm sick of being spoken to in English...always in English. I want my child to grow up among Québécois...real Québécois.

LUIGI: *(Ironic.)* Oh, we'll protect him, my love, never fear... We'll make sure he won't be contaminated... We'll keep him away from the Romanos and the Romanovs, the Nguyens and the Gomez, the Dimitris and the destitute. I promise you...our child will be perfect, he won't have an accent, he'll grow up hating the English, the poor, and the immigrants...

Scene 10

> *Italy, late 1980s. NINO and MARIA on the balcony.*
> *A bird-cage hangs from a hook.*
>
> *Swallows...chirping in the cage...*
>
> *Rolling thunder in the distance...*

NINO: A swallow...a dead swallow...I found it by the stream.

MARIA: It was right here, on this balcony, that your father used to catch birds and then he'd put them in this cage.

NINO: That was my favourite story when I was little.

MARIA: Your father was happy here. There were still people in the village and at dusk the sky was full of birds.

NINO: I want to leave...I don't want to stay here... I've had it with this abandoned village, this deathly silence, these houses: with their doors and windows bashed in, they're like gigantic skulls... I want to go home...see my friends... I haven't got anybody here... Where's my father?...If he doesn't want to go home with me I'll go by myself...

> *The storm is coming closer, the thunder is louder.*

MARIA: We've been waiting so long for you, your grandfather and I. You can't do that to us.

NINO: I can't? In fifteen years you didn't come to see me even once, and now you say I can't do that to you? You, Nonna, at least you could have come...Why didn't you?

MARIA: I couldn't leave your Nonno all alone.

NINO: That's not true... I don't believe you... You didn't come because I didn't matter enough to you...

MARIA: Look! Look at the swallow up there, on the church steeple...she won't live for long now that she's alone.

We hear the thunder getting louder and louder.

Look, now there's hail! It's going to destroy everything...

Bells start ringing,

Go and help your grandfather ring the bells.

The bells continue to ring.

The storm passes over the village.

Musc resolves.

Scene 11

NINO and FRANCO inside the church steeple during the storm.

FRANCO: You can stop now, the storm is over.

NINO: It worked! We did it! I want to see the bells up close, Grandpa, I want to touch them.

FRANCO: The staircase is behind us. I'll wait for you here.

NINO: I want you to come up with me.

FRANCO: You go first, I'll be right behind you.

They climb creaky wooden staircase to the top...

NINO: Have you ever gone up to the top?

FRANCO: Once.

NINO: With Papa?

FRANCO: It was before he was born.

NINO: I'll bring him tomorrow.

FRANCO: A few more steps and we're there.

Scene 11a

NINO and FRANCO on top of steeple...

Light chilly wind playing off bells...

NINO running his hands on the bells...

NINO: I can see the bells...there's three of them...one is taller than me... This is so high! You can see so far! The clouds...I can practically touch the clouds. Nonno, your village looks like a Christmas crèche, it's so small. I can see your house. The one with the big chimney. Look...look at the plaque... It's got your name on it. The priest thanks you for saving...what did you save, Nonno? I can't read the last word. What's that word? You're shivering, Nonno. Here, come inside. What was it you saved?

FRANCO: It doesn't matter now.

NINO: You look dizzy, Nonno...sit down...sit down...

FRANCO: I never should have come up here.

NINO: What did you save? Why are you so pale?

FRANCO: It was so long ago!

            Music resolves.

FRANCO: I wanted to show them... I wanted to show them that they didn't scare me...

NINO: Who? You're shivering more and more.

FRANCO: We couldn't go on like that... I feel cold all of a sudden...

NINO: There's a draft here...come and stand behind the pillar...

FRANCO: They'd been terrorizing us for so long...we had to...

NINO: *(Interrupts him.)* ...give me your hands, I'll warm them up...

FRANCO: ...for once somebody had to tell them, No...that's why I came up here. Everything was so sad. On winter nights, when the wind came rushing into the narrow lanes you could hear the village cry.

NINO: Take my shirt, put it over your shoulders...I'm not cold...

FRANCO: They wanted to take away the bells to make cannons.

NINO: There, now you won't be cold.

             Music: "Memory of Maria's Pain"....under...

FRANCO: It's so peaceful! It's never so peaceful as after a storm...not one sound...no dogs barking...even the cicadas are quiet...like it was that night...just after sunset...the streets were deserted...all the lights were out...the shutters closed...the moon hiding behind a cloud...everyone knew that the blackshirts were coming...they were coming to kill the village and take away its music...for so long, they raped the women and humiliated the men...the day they came to steal the bells I took my father's rifle and came up here...in the distance I could hear their boots and the leaders yelling orders...just as they were crossing the main square I fired two shots...they stopped for a moment, then they started marching again...there were fifty of them, all in black...like crows...when they bashed in the door of the church, I rang the bells so loud you could hear them all over the region...right away the villages emptied out and a flood of farmers came up from the valley and drove away the crows, singing.

             Music is featured for a brief pause in the dialogue...

             The next morning, I found Maria. She was crying and her dress was torn.

             FRANCO races down from the church steeple.

NINO: Wait, Nonno, let me go down first...lean on me...

NINO follows...

Music is featured for a while then resolves before next scene starts...

Scene 12

Italy, late 1980s. DANIELLE and LUIGI, then NINO. On the balcony.

Summer cicadas at their hottest.

DANIELLE: I came for Nino...it was very hard to get here...the road to the village is in such terrible shape... I didn't meet a single car...there's no one anywhere...all I could hear was the braying of a donkey... That's the saddest sound, the sound of a braying donkey...I still have goose-flesh... *(Brief pause.)* I feel dizzy...it must be the heat...I'm parched...give me some water...

LUIGI holds out a pitcher. She pours water over her head, then she drinks.

It tastes of sulphur just like it did fifteen years ago...this heat!... I'd forgotten how hot it can get...you haven't said a word...it's been so long since we've had a conversation... *(Brief pause.)* We had a son...we stayed together nearly five years...we did have some wonderful moments ...

LUIGI: *(Ironic.)* Demonstrations, handing out tracts, fights with the cops...and meetings, meetings, meetings...

DANIELLE: It was what we believed in. We had ideals. We thought we could change so many things.

LUIGI: We were positive we had the recipe for a perfect society, but we didn't have the one for living as a couple.

DANIELLE: Too many things came between us…

LUIGI: The same things that led us to live together.

DANIELLE: You were so different from anyone I'd known…
              You fascinated me…but then, over time, I couldn't
              stand hearing you say that my party was one-third
              racists, one-third petty bourgeois reactionaries and
              the rest a bunch of power-hungry opportunists.

LUIGI: I beg your forgiveness… I think I was mistaken
              about the proportions.

DANIELLE: *(Taking the blow.)* You never tried to understand
              why the cause I was fighting for was so important to
              me…it never occurred to you that it could be just as
              legitimate as yours…when I think that you accused
              me of wanting to divide the working class…the
              Canadian working class…

LUIGI: You never really loved me…after your trips to Cuba
              in solidarity with the proletariat, your stint in a poor
              neighbourhood as a contrite member of the
              bourgeoisie, the next trendy thing was to spend
              time with an immigrant…any immigrant…so you
              could atone for generations of xenophobia.

DANIELLE: You're wrong…I loved you…I loved you so much,
              I've never been able to live with another man.

LUIGI: You, with one other man? You always need several
              men at the same time…

DANIELLE: You're reproaching me for something that was
              always fine for you. *(Brief pause.)* Where's Nino?
              How did he manage to spend two weeks here? Go
              and look for him. I want to leave as soon as I can.
              We'll spend two days in Venice, then go home. I've
              got a lot of work to do—work that can't wait.

LUIGI: Another election?

DANIELLE: I resigned from the party. I'm running my father's company now. He had a heart attack two days after you left...

LUIGI: *(Mocking and contemptuous.)* Your father's company...your father's company... Is that all that's left of your ideals?... Is that the country you were dreaming of?... The people you wanted to liberate?... The two hundred years of history you wanted to avenge?... Is that all that's left?...A house-cleaning company...fifty immigrants with their dust-rags going to work every morning for starvation wages?... *(Mocking laugh.)* Instead of liberating your country you've decided to clean it?

DANIELLE: I did my share...when I look around me...when I see how far we've come, I'm happy about what's been accomplished...and we could have done a lot more if there hadn't been people like you to denigrate us...to call us backward and vindictive and racist...

Scene 12a

NINO runs up stone steps...

Swallow chirping in bird cage...

NINO: I caught the swallow...I caught it for Nonna and Nonno... *(Sees his mother.)* Mamma? You're here already?

DANIELLE: You asked me to come so I came.

NINO: Yes, but not so soon ...

DANIELLE: I had to change my plans...I was so anxious to get here...I never should have let your father bring you to this place...fifteen years ago there were still a few people...and then the heat... I've come to get you...we'll go home as soon as we can... I've got big news... Before I left I bought a wonderful house right next door to your friend Olivier... There's a

| | sound system and a home theatre in the basement and I had a skateboard ramp built right next to the pool... Wait till you see the pool... |

NINO: *(Interrupts his mother.)* ...there's a house here, next to the church...the one with a plane tree out front...if it's too small we'll find a bigger one...there are so many empty houses...I saw another one too that's very big...from the balcony you can see the whole valley...we can walk around the village if you want and choose one together...if you're too tired, Mamà, we can go later...or tomorrow...

DANIELLE: Tomorrow I'd like to get off to an early start.

NINO: I'm not leaving till I find another swallow. I don't want this one to die.

DANIELLE: You spent last summer with your father, you have to spend this one with me.

LUIGI: *(To NINO.)* She wanted to spend last summer with her new lover.

DANIELLE: What about you, who did you spend all those years with when you hardly saw your son?

LUIGI: You're the one who wouldn't let me see him, even though you left him with a sitter every other night.

DANIELLE: With you it would've been every night.

NINO: Enough! That's enough! Go away both of you... I don't want to be with either one of you... Why did you have me if you didn't want to take care of me? Why? *(Leaves, running.)*

LUIGI: Where are you going, Nino? Wait for me.

Scene 13

Italy, late 1980s. NINO and LUIGI on the church bell tower.

Light whistling wind…

We hear the small bells ring several times.

LUIGI: Who showed you how to climb onto the steeple?

NINO: Nonno…he's the one who saved the bells…you can read it right here, on the plaque.

LUIGI: He never told me about that.

NINO: Look at all the empty villages! Why did you all go away? You should have climbed up on the steeples… You'd have seen there's enough room for everybody… You should've done like grandpa… That's why he came back …

LUIGI: You can't imagine…you've never lived on this hill.

NINO: What didn't you have here? What was it that didn't exist here?

LUIGI: We all need to go far away so each of us can discover that he's bigger than his village…

NINO: Imagine, Papa…

Music "Imagine This Village Full of People."

…imagine this village full of people…like when you were little…Imagine that I was born here…today we'd be celebrating the Patron Saint with music and fireworks…the stream wouldn't be poisoned…and up in the sky would be hundreds of swallows …imagine…we'd live next door to Nonna and Nonno…you and Mamà and me, we'd have been living in the same house for fifteen years…we'd be together every morning…every evening…you and me and Mamma…you and me and mamà…

LUIGI: *(Beat.)* It's getting late…let's go down…

Swallow approaching then landing on bells…

NINO: A swallow! A swallow! Look, it's landed on one of the bells...I have to catch it.

Music is featured and bridges to next scene...

Scene 14

Italy, late 1980s. FRANCO, MARIA, LUIGI...and at the very end, NINO.

LUIGI: I'm leaving tomorrow.

FRANCO: With Nino?

LUIGI: Yes, with Nino.

FRANCO heads for the door.

Why are you leaving? I'm your son...I'm with you here... We may never see each other again...

MARIA: Let's leave with him.

FRANCO: Where he's going is no place for us... Over there we'll always be outsiders... Our home is here.

MARIA: Our home is where Nino and Luigi are.

FRANCO: I won't let this village die...it won't die before I do.

LUIGI: You were away for so long...there were still people here when you left...when there were people living in the houses ...

FRANCO: That was why I went away... Whenever I went outside people insulted me. At first they were all glad that I'd been able to save the bells...they even carried me through the village in triumph... They didn't know yet about how the crows had soiled my dove... As soon as they found out, they went wild and blamed me. They kept saying again and again that I knew Maria had been raped by the blackshirts and that I'd been afraid to defend her. I didn't know...I didn't know...I believed she was safe...

They called me a coward...they called me crazy...the village children came and shouted it under my window over and over again every day... I didn't know... *(Brief pause.)* To get my revenge I took Maria to the church and married her...I didn't want her to have to hide all her life like Tina and Giovanna and Silvia...abandoned by their fiancés... Nobody came to the wedding...people closed their shutters when we walked by...they threw mud at her white dress...and the only person at the church was the priest... This village is so much better since all the people have gone.

> *Music: "Memory of Maria's Pain"...reprise under...*

MARIA: Tomorrow morning I'll put on my veil and my white dress and you'll take me to the church and marry me again, now that there's no one to mock us...and then we'll leave.

FRANCO: Me, I'm staying ...

MARIA: I won't be able to love you if we aren't with Nino and Luigi.

FRANCO: You did for fifteen years ...

MARIA: I'd have left before if they'd come for me.

NINO: *(Running, holding the cage with two swallows in it.)* I caught another swallow, up there, on the steeple...now they're going to live...and more swallows are going to come ...

> *Music is featured and resolves....*

Scene 15

> *Italy, late 1980s. LUIGI, DANIELLE, NINO, then FRANCO and MARIA.*
>
> *Hot day-time ambience.*

DANIELLE: Time to go, Nino.

NINO: I'm staying in the village with Nonno and Nonna.

LUIGI: They're going to leave too.

NINO: Grandpa will never leave his village again.

DANIELLE: We're your parents...you have to come home with us...

NINO: I haven't got parents...parents who don't love each other aren't parents...you've never cared about me...you've never understood me...I needed the two of you...the two of you together...you knew that was what I wanted...but you never listened to me...you had so many things to do...so many things that were more important than me...more important than us...

> *Music: "The Journey Back"—reprise, but mingles in with the voices and the music and the voices become one...*
>
> *FRANCO and MARIA appear.*

FRANCO: I'm staying.

MARIA: We're leaving.

DANIELLE: I'm not leaving without Nino.

LUIGI: Let's all go!

FRANCO: I'm not leaving.

MARIA: I won't go without you.

NINO: Let's stay! Let's all of us stay!

> *All the adults speak at the same time and their sentences overlap, creating a genuine cacophony.*

FRANCO: Let's stay here!

LUIGI: Let's leave!

NINO: But all of us together...anywhere, as long as we're together ...

Church bells toll the time.

Music is featured for a while then held for credits...

The End.

Joy Geen
(See You Again)

JOHN NG

John Ng

John Ng has lived in Ottawa since immigrating to Canada from Hong Kong at the age of nine. He is a graduate of the University of Ottawa with a B.A. in Theatre with Honours in Directing.

In 1994, with local native writer and multi-media artist Morris Isaac, John assisted in the creation of *Thanks to Peter*, a play about friendship between two aboriginal boys struggling in foster care. The play was also staged and produced by At Your Own Risk Productions in Ottawa, a company co-founded by John and four fellow graduates from the University of Ottawa Theatre Programme.

Two-and-a-half years ago, John decided to focus more on playwriting. This effort resulted in his first play, a one-act piece entitled *I*, on which *Joy Geen* is based and produced at the 2001 Toronto Fringe Festival. He is currently a member of the NAC-GCTC playwrights unit in Ottawa and is developing a play based on the life of Larry Kwong, the first player in the NHL of Asian descent.

About the Play

Over the past few years, the headlines have screamed about illegal shiploads of Chinese immigrants besieging our west coast, but very rarely have the news stories probed into the lives people desperate enough to risk such a dangerous voyage. In *Joy Geen* (which is Cantonese for "See you again"), John Ng goes behind scenes, and tells the story of Shu Ming, who boards a freighter and is smuggled into Canada by a Chinese entrepreneur, the Snakehead. Shu Ming has only one contact in Canada—a family from her village in China who have built up a successful business in Toronto. When she seeks them out they are forced to decide where their lives begin and end, and where their duties and obligations to a friend from their parents' village in China extend.

Cast

SHU MING WAH: .... Mung-Ling Tsui

MAGGIE: .... Jean Yoon

JASON: .... Richard Lee

KARIN: .... Marjorie Chan

SNAKEHEAD: .... Ho Chow

DIM SUM/VILLAGE WOMAN: .... Margaret Ma

FATHER: .... William Johnson

VILLAGE MAN: .... John Ng

IMMIGRATION OFFCER: .... Shannon Lawson

Production Credits

Producer/Director: .... Linda Grearson

Associate Producer: .... Colleen Wooods

Original Music: .... Donald Quan

Script Editor: .... Dave Carley

Recording Engineer: .... Wayne Richards

Sound Effects: .... Matt Wilcott

Scene 1
Int. Shu Ming

        Waves crashing against a rocky shore, cross fade to:

        Theme composition, fade to:

SHU MING: *(Narr.)* I know it is difficult for people to understand, but please don't tell me if you were in my position you would not have done the same thing.

Scene 2
Int. Snakehead Addresses Audience

        Music: "Snakehead Theme."

SNAKE: *(Overlap.) Teng jew lay: Aw mo jo chaw yaer* (Listen to me: I haven't done anything wrong)…I'm a saviour, not a crook. I'm the Chinese Santa Claus. My gift is to help those who can't help themselves. I don't hold a gun to anybody's head. People come to me for a way to a better life. I do what I can. Sure, there are risks. But when you buy fresh meat from your butcher, or you walk across the middle of a busy street, there are risks there too. Nothing is guaranteed. What is so wrong, anyway? These migrants want to work. That's why they come here. They're not like those other refugees who are happy just to feed off the government. Those are the ones you should go after—the people out looking for a free ride…

        Music out.

Scene 3
Int. Large Chinese Restaurant

Noisy ambience inside crowded dining room (chatter, bustling activity, etc.) under.

JASON: *(Calling to Dim Sum Woman.)* Phone Jawl!...Yuaw Mo Phone Jawl-ah? (Chicken feet!...You have any chicken feet?)

DIM SUM
WOMAN: *(From a distance.)* My-sye-la! Siu-mai, yiew-mm-yiew! (Sold out! Pork dumpling, you want it!)

JASON: *Mmm-yiew-ah! Mut do-mmm-yeiw-ah!...*(Don't want it! Don't want anything!)

Returns to table.

Chee-chee doo-hai gum-geh...(It's always like this) There are hundreds of *Dim Sum* places in Toronto— I don't know why we keep coming back here. Whenever you want something, they never have it.

MAGGIE: Jason, would you please just let me finish?

KARIN: I'm still listening, Maggie.

MAGGIE: Thank you, Karin.

KARIN: What else did Aunt Wei say?

Letter being shuffled in MAGGIE's hands.

MAGGIE: *(She reads.)* "You know the desperate situation we're in...the Flower Man has offered us twelve hundred yuan to take little Fong away and work for him in the city. If we accept, I am afraid we would not see our granddaughter again. But we already owe the village chief five hundred... Everyone knows you are a generous and kind person. Please have pity on us...Can you help?"

KARIN: That's so sad. We *are* going to help them, right?

JASON: Help them? We should just tell them the truth.

MAGGIE: What?

JASON: Tell them Ah-Ma is no longer with us, so stop sending us these endless requests for a handout.

MAGGIE: You know it's not that simple.

JASON: Why not? It's been over a year. Don't you think it's time we drop this charade we're playing, acting like she's still here?

MAGGIE: It's not the kind of news Ah-Ma's family would take very well—

JASON: I'm sure they'll get over it.

KARIN: That's not the point.

JASON: What's that?

MAGGIE: Jason.

JASON: Oh, so now you're going to tell us what that is, right?

MAGGIE: That's enough. *(Pause.)* Ah-Ma would not want our relatives to find out she passed away so soon. Many of them are elderly and have counted on her support for so long. It would be wrong to do anything to upset them now.

JASON: But it's OK for them to take advantage of *us.* They had Mom and Dad on a string for as long as we can remember. Now they're both gone, you want to take over like nothing's happened. How do we even know what they're saying in that letter is true? What if they're only using our money to pay off gambling debts? Have you thought of that?

KARIN: I'm sorry, but I think you're over-exaggerating just a little bit there.

JASON: Am I? Look what happened to Ah-Cho when he

went back to China. Relatives he had never heard of kept showing up, just waiting for him to open his wallet. He showed me these pictures of his family's place in the village, and all you notice is this giant TV screen sitting there, taking up half the room. I said, 'Cho, you never told me your family was rich?' He says, 'They're not. It just looks that way.' This is what they expect now. You call that fair?

KARIN: So Ah-Cho is generous with his family. What's wrong with that? Maybe you could learn something from him.

MAGGIE: Karin.

JASON: *Learn* something? Let them come over here and spend a week with him washing dishes in our crappy restaurant. See how much fun they learn.

KARIN: It must be so gratifying, isn't it, knowing that you're always right.

JASON: What do you know? You really think they give a damn about us?

KARIN: We're talking about our Mom's family here.

JASON: Enough is enough. We don't owe them a thing.

MAGGIE: We will help Aunt Wei and Uncle Tse... With or without you.

Chair pushed back from table.

JASON: Forget it. *(Gets up.)* I'm outta here. You want to be the boss, go ahead. Have it your way...

JASON walks away as dim sum cart is being pushed closer.

DIM SUM
WOMAN: *(Moving in.) Hey, phone Jawl-ah! Phone Jawl dou-la!* (Hey, chicken feet! Chicken feet is here now!) Where is he going? He wanted chicken feet—Now he's not

here! How many do you want?

KARIN: Ah… No, thanks.

                Out.

Scene 4
Int. Snakehead Addresses Audience

                Music: "Snakehead Theme."

SNAKE: This much is true: Chinese people are not lazy. We earn everything that we have. 'Work ethic' is our middle name. You want to pay us small wages—no problem. We don't complain. We just work longer and eat less. You won't see us argue or cause any trouble. Isn't that what you want? Immigrants who don't make any noise? We know how it is. Let's face it, where would your country be today without cheap Chinese labour… Am I right?

                Music fade out.

Scene 5
Ext. Cemetery in the City

                A few birds.

                Light traffic in distance, under.

KARIN: How many incense sticks should I pull, Maggie?

MAGGIE: Three. It's always three. One for heaven, one for earth, and one for the wandering—

KARIN: Spirit… Right, of course, I knew that.

MAGGIE: Ah-huh…

KARIN: To be honest, I always thought three was just a lucky number.

MAGGIE: It is. That's why it's important we do it right.

KARIN: You know, somehow I was never able to get Mom to explain all this ritual stuff to me.

MAGGIE: It's not the kind of thing we're supposed to talk about. You learn by watching, not from questioning at everything.

KARIN: Well, I guess I wasn't a very good learner then.

MAGGIE: I'm sure Ah-Ma forgives you.

KARIN: (*Lets out a laugh.*)

MAGGIE: What Is it?

KARIN: I'm sorry…It's just I remember Mom's favourite expression was, 'Never forgive and don't ever forget.'

MAGGIE: Hmm…

KARIN: You're still upset, aren't you? What was it Mom used to call Jason, 'A wooden post with two ears?' Maybe we should just go on ahead. I doubt if he'll show up now.

MAGGIE: He was right.

KARIN: Sorry?

MAGGIE: He's got a point.

KARIN: *Jason?* But, Maggie…

MAGGIE: As much as I feel for the relatives back home, sometimes I do feel like we're being taken advantage of.

KARIN: Jason doesn't know what he's talking about. He only cares about himself.

MAGGIE: That's not true. And I wish you wouldn't say things like that about your big brother.

KARIN: Well, I'm just saying…

MAGGIE: If you read some of the letters they used to send Ah-
                Ma, you'd wonder too where they get the idea we're
                so well off.

KARIN: Aren't we though? I mean...really.

MAGGIE: Yes, we are much luckier than they are, but it didn't
                come without a price.

KARIN: You're not saying we should just forget about them?
                Whenever I think about our family back home, what
                they have to go through, I say to myself, it could
                easily be me instead of them. If Daddy didn't have a
                cousin with a restaurant to sponsor him over, I
                probably wouldn't even be standing here right now.

MAGGIE: Karin...

KARIN: But it takes so little for us just to make a difference.
                And isn't that something Mom would want?

                Fade up to Chinese festival music.

MAGGIE: Yes. Keep the happy thoughts...and try to take care
                of those who still need her. *(Pause.)* OK, go ahead,
                light the incense.

                A match is lit, quickly to:

Scene 6
Ext. Shu Ming's Village, Guangdong Province, China

                Chinese festival music.

                Firecrackers ignite in the air.

                *A village gathering. Merriment with children
                laughing and playing, under:*

SNAKE: *(Playing the crowd.) Ney dey quaw ley tigh ah-la!* (You
                all come have a look at this!) They say a picture can
                tell a thousand words. Well, then, I let you be the
                judge. Look at what you've all been missing...

SHU MING: *(Narr.)* It was like a festival. The whole village had gathered together to meet the man they called Big Uncle. He arrived with pictures from the West for everyone to see. He introduced himself as a travel agent for the common people. He said he could take anybody anywhere—for a price, of course.

SNAKE: See this. This is premium American whiskey. You can't find this here even if you tried. Smell the fragrance. *(He sniffs.)* It's beautiful. Here, my friend, let me pour you some. Don't be shy. It's good for you.

> *Laughter from FATHER and SNAKEHEAD.*

FATHER: *(In background.) Dor-jeh, dor-jeh...* (Thank-you, thank-you.)

SHU MING: *(Narr.)* It was the first time I met the Snakehead. I had heard rumours about who he was, and all the connections he had, but I still didn't know what to expect. I remember my father, grinning from ear to ear. When he ushered me aside to look at a photograph the Snakehead had given him, I knew right away, the man was the answer to his prayers.

FATHER: *Shu-Ming...quaw ley.* (Shu Ming, come this way.) Look here...look at this one of Niagara Falls.

> *Out.*

> *Music: "Shu Ming's Theme."*

Scene 6A
Int. Shu Ming's Narration

SHU MING: *(Narr.)* I dreamed of seeing the falls ever since Godmother sent us pictures taken of her family there. When they left the village to go to Canada, I thought we would be joining them too. I thought that's what happens to every family sooner or later. You wait like everyone else until it is your turn to go to Gold Mountain. You go. You make a lot of money. And you come back to build a big house, have two German dogs and a Rolls Royce to drive around. That's what I thought. But our turn never came. When we received news that Godmother had given birth to baby Karin, I asked Father if we would some day get the chance to see the little girl with the strange name. He said quietly, 'No...

FATHER: *Ah-nueh, mmm ho lum gum daw-la* (Daughter, try not to think about it.) ...We cannot wish for much. Your Godmother and her family...they are Canadians now.

SHU MING: *(Narr.)* I knew what he meant: I would never get to grow up with them. It didn't seem fair to me. Father wouldn't let on that our application to immigrate had been rejected because we were considered too poor and didn't have enough skills or education. He was so ashamed...

               Out.

Scene 6B
Ext. Shu Ming's Village

               Sounds of village people gathering under:

FATHER: This is my daughter here. She is all I have to my name. Her mother has passed on. I have no son. No face. What is there for her here?

SNAKE: Then allow me to open the door.

FATHER: How can you help us?

SNAKE: If you are willing to make the sacrifices, fortune will come your way. Your ancestors are not blind; their eyes in heaven can see that you deserve much more. Your daughter is still young. And with a face like that, I don't have to tell you...she will make you proud.

SHU MING: *(Narr.)* The man could've been selling dog manure and Father would have bought it for its weight in gold. You don't argue with your father. This was the only way...

> *Voices of villagers clamouring over one another to speak.*
>
> *Music: Sneak in and fade up to "The Journey Begins."*

WOMAN: *Yut phan phone schien...Man zhu zing yee* (All's well and Godspeed.) We are counting on you, *Ah-Ming*...You don't forget us now...

MAN: Ah-Ming is a good girl... She would never disappoint us...

> *Out.*

Scene 7
Ext. The Journey Begins

> *Music: "The Journey Begins."*

SHU MING: *(Narr.)* All our relatives and friends in the village got together to help. We had enough to pay for half the ticket up front. I would work for the Snakehead to pay off the rest. It seemed like such a simple plan at the time...

> *Footsteps hurrying along wooden planks.*
>
> *Human voices scattered in all directions.*
>
> *Waves washing against boat.*
>
> *Seagulls loitering about, cross fade to:*
>
> *Boat drifting in ocean, under.*

(Narr.) You can't imagine what it was like on the boat... They herded us inside a storage compartment below deck. We weren't allowed to

carry any luggage, only the clothes we wore and nothing more. They gave us rations of sticky rice and a plastic bottle filled with water. In the corner was a large wooden bucket. We all knew what was ahead of us...

A child crying in need.

(Narr.) The children...You could hear them but what could you do...After a while, you shut your ears out and you say to yourself, it doesn't matter. They can cry all they want. We're in here for the same reasons. They have to suffer just like the rest of us.

Crying stops.

(Narr.) It was so dark...soon the smell of our waste became almost unbearable...it was hard to breathe...the whole time I tried to sleep. I forced myself to think of good thoughts...of seeing Godmother...Maggie and Jason...little Karin...

Boat in ocean out.

House door opens from the inside, quickly to:

Out.

Scene 8
Int. Shu Ming's Fantasy—Her Arrival

SIBLINGS: *Shu Ming! Nay-Ho!* (Hello!)

MAGGIE: It *is* you—I must be dreaming!

KARIN: I knew you'd be here—it's déja vu, isn't it?

JASON: Twenty-five years it's been—yet look at you—you still look like a ten-year old!

MAGGIE: Do you remember the anthem we had to sing every morning in the schoolyard when we were kids?

JASON: *(Jovial.)* Oh, gee, Maggie! You have to remind us—
            Now I won't be able to get that stupid song out of
            my head!

MAGGIE: Remember how we used to mess up the lyrics?

KARIN: I'd like to hear it. Can you sing me a few bars?

MAGGIE: *(Laughs.)* You don't want to get us started—right,
            Shu Ming?

KARIN: *Please...*

JASON: Don't forget to march—and raise your fist high in
            the air.

            MAGGIE and JASON begin to sing off-key.

KARIN: *(Can't contain her laughter.)* Oh, my god, that's so
            funny!

MAGGIE: Come, Ah-Ma... Look who's here—look who's
            finally made it?

JASON: It's little Shu Ming...

ALL: We're so happy you're here!

Scene 9
Ext. The Journey of the Boat

            Journey on the boat.

SHU MING: *(Narr.)*   I think we were at sea for over ninety
            days...

            Boat drifting in ocean.

            (Narr.) It seemed like it was never going to end.
            When the storm hit, I thought it was all over...

            Thunder and lightning.

            Fierce wind.

Heavy waves slamming against ship.

(*Narr.*) We were crammed out on to the deck. Cold and wet. We could see land ahead in front of us...

Fear and panic on board ship; voices yelling above confusion, under.

People abandoning ship; diving into shallow water.

(*Narr.*) People started jumping overboard...I could see some of them swimming to shore...I thought about escaping...

Storm fades.

(*Narr.*) But then everything just stopped. The sky began to clear...The air smelled fresh and clean...I could see trees everywhere. It was like waking up in a dream, it looked so beautiful.

Coast guard ship with siren approaches from distance.

(*Narr.*) I waded through shallow water and sat on a rock by the shore, too numb to go any farther. As I was catching my breath, I saw the patrol boat coming closer. I began to repeat over and over in my head what the Snakehead had instructed me to tell the authorities in the event we were caught. I was terrified. What if they could tell that I'm lying? What if they didn't care at all? I can't be sent back home with nothing to show for. How can I face my father and everyone in the village then? I need to learn it well and quickly... My name is *Wah Shu Ming*...

Out.

Scene 10
Int. Shu Ming's Reality—Her Arrival at Immigration
Detention Centre

Loud buzzer.

Automatic security door opening.

Footsteps moving along concrete floor.

OFFICER: Wah Shu Ming.

SHU MING: (*With accent.*) Yes…Wah Shu Ming.

OFFICER: Ms. Wah, we have considered your case and a decision has been made to move forward with your refugee claim. Your fear of persecution from the Public Security Bureau in China as a result of your participation in a demonstration against the government appears credible and consistent with the documentary evidence. Therefore, we are granting you a full review before the Immigration and Refugee Board. An adjudicator will decide your case at a full hearing to be set for a later date. If the decision is positive, you will obtain refugee status and can apply for permanent residence in Canada. (*Fade under SNAKEHEAD's following lines.*)

SNAKEHEAD: Don't act scared. They can sense fear. Don't say anything. Wait until they ask you.

OFFICER: Wait—if, however, the decision is negative, you will be entitled to apply for the appeal process to be reviewed by the Federal Court. But for now, the first order is for you to attend the hearing before the Board. Do you understand?

SHU MING: Ah yes…

OFFICER: An individual is here on your behalf from the local Vancouver Chinese community. He has come forward and is prepared to act as your guarantor and pay the security deposit to ensure your availability when required. This person has declared that he is related to your family.

SHU MING: Yes…he is a distant uncle.

OFFICER: Alright. Here's the good news, Ms. Wah…we are recommending that you be released into your uncle's care pending notification of your refugee hearing. In assessing your case, we've determined that you will not pose as a flight risk or a danger to the public during this period of review. Further detention, therefore, will not be justified. You must, however, adhere to all conditions under the terms of your release. Do you understand?

SHU MING: Yes…thank you.

OFFICER: Very well. Do you have any further questions?

SHU MING: No.

Loud buzzer.

Scene 11
Int. Inside Cabin of Truck Travelling East Along Trans-Canada Highway, Near the Manitoba-Ontario Border

Snakehead theme…

Highway traffic noise in background.

Tractor-trailer passes by.

Cabin rattling over bumpy road, under.

SHU MING: Where are we going?

SNAKE: What do *you* care? You should be grateful we got you out.

SHU MING: I just want to know where you're taking me.

SNAKE: You have a huge debt to pay, and it's growing by the minute.

SHU MING: But I thought—

SNAKE: You thought *what*—you're going to go back for your court hearing? If that's what you're thinking, you really are as stupid as you look.

SHU MING: I thought you were taking me to Toronto.

SNAKE: Shut your mouth! I'll take you wherever I want. You don't get to pick and choose here, little girl.

SHU MING: I need to go to Toronto. I have—

SNAKE: You have nothing! Where are you going to go? You came here on a one-way ticket, get it through your thick head.

SHU MING: I don't want to run anymore.

SNAKE: You expect a refund! Go cry to Uncle Sam, because that's where you're heading. There's a boat waiting at the Indian Reserve. You got that? It's going to get wet. Be prepared to swim.

                 SHU MING sobbing underneath.

              Look at you. How pathetic. You're looking for a bruise on that old face of yours.

                 Truck slowing down.

              I'll fill up. Stay in here and don't try anything stupid. Wipe your face clean before I come back.

                 Highway and traffic noises fade out.

Scene 12
Ext. Shu Ming's Escape

                 SHU MING's escape—frantic movement, under.

                 SHU MING's running footsteps and heavy breathing.

Highway traffic coming and going, follow by street noise of downtown Toronto (streetcars, cabs honking, pedestrians, etc.).

OFFICER: ...You will not pose as a flight risk or a danger to the public...

SNAKE: ...You have nothing! Where are you going to go?...

FATHER: Be a good daughter and do as they tell you, Shu Ming...

SHU MING: I don't want to run anymore... Please...help me...where are you...

Out.

Scene 13
Int. The Lau's Home

Door bell rings.

Door opens.

Music out.

MAGGIE: Oh, my god! *Shu Ming!* What are you doing here?

Scene 14
Int. The Lau's Restaurant

Light restaurant ambience.

A near-empty small dining room with a running goldfish tank, under.

KARIN: Would you like to go see the falls?

SHU MING: I...

JASON: It's really over-rated—and passé.

KARIN: Don't listen to him. We can go whenever you like—how about tomorrow?

SHU MING: That would be nice—

JASON: Shu Ming just got here. Let her relax.

KARIN: You must have a list of places you're just dying to go see.

SHU MING: Well—

KARIN: I can name a few places in China I wouldn't mind visiting. There's the Yangzte…Tiannanmen Square, and oh, of course, the Great Wall.

JASON: I've always wanted to take a bat and ball and go hit a few over the Wall.

MAGGIE coming through swinging kitchen door.

MAGGIE: *(Approaching.)* Here we are. Have some tea, Shu Ming.

SHU MING: Thank you…your restaurant is very nice.

MAGGIE: It pays the bills. That's all we ask.

SHU MING: Where is Godmother?

MAGGIE: Ahhh…

KARIN: *(Jumps in quickly.)*You must be tired, Shu Ming. How was the flight over?

SHU MING: Ahhh…

KARIN: *(Continues.)* You know, Jason's afraid to fly. When they came over he got so airsick he used up every paper bag on the plane. Isn't that right, big brother?

JASON: *(Dragged in.)* Yes. An airplane is no place to introduce a nine-year old to seaweed udon for the first time.

KARIN: *(Sharing a secret.)* He can't stand Japanese food…

SHU MING: Oh, I see...

JASON: If you let her, Karin could talk until your ears get
              swollen.

KARIN: I took a course to learn to speak Mandarin.

SHU MING: Mandarin...wonderful.

JASON: Oh great, here it comes.

KARIN: *Wor yewh e dien lah-jiew jieng cheu wor duk chow mein.*
              (I would like some hot sauce for my fried noodles.)

SHU MING: *Chow mein...*

JASON: That's very impressive, little sister. You know how
              to order hot sauce for your fried noodles.

KARIN: I'll be ready when I go to China.

JASON: Don't expect *me* to fly with you.

KARIN: I'm all set, as soon as I graduate next spring.

SHU MING: Congratulations...

JASON: Go on, brag about your little piece of paper.

KARIN: I'm not.

JASON: Why don't you just tell us what you're going to be
              doing in China, Karin?

KARIN: Well, wait. OK, it's this: First, I want to discover and
              connect with my roots.

JASON: And—

KARIN: And learn more about my ancestral heritage...

JASON: And—

KARIN: Bit of sightseeing... *I'm so excited!*

JASON: And—

KARIN: I'm *getting* to it.

JASON: Because you—

KARIN: Because I...

JASON: Want to—

KARIN: I'm going to—

JASON: She wants to save the panda bear.

KARIN: Well, yes! Actually, I'm going to be doing some field research with the World Centre for the Reproduction of Endangered Species.

JASON: Good luck.

KARIN: It's a global cause.

JASON: So is world hunger.

KARIN: What?

JASON: There're over a billion people in China, why don't you go do something about that? Who gives a damn about the panda? They're nothing more than a bunch of overweight and undersexed raccoons.

KARIN: Why does it sound like you're criticizing me for the career I've chosen for myself? You know, I can't help it if you never graduated from your so-called, 'Five-year plan.'

JASON: That's brilliant. I was wondering how long it would take before you made that public announcement. Tell me, you think I went to university so I could become a waiter for the rest of my life? I never finished because I had to look after the restaurant while you were running around like a spoiled brat.

MAGGIE: Jason, please.

KARIN: You're way too bitter.

JASON: I live with you, don't I?

KARIN:	You're *so* wrong for the service industry.
JASON:	I'm always right—*remember?*
KARIN:	Forget it, I'm not talking to you.
JASON:	Promise?
KARIN:	Grow up.
JASON:	You first.
KARIN:	You're a real…
JASON:	Say it.
KARIN:	No.
JASON:	Say what's on your mind.
KARIN:	I won't!
JASON:	Spit it out!
KARIN:	You can't make me.
SHU MING:	Please, Maggie. Where is Godmother?
MAGGIE:	She's ah…
JASON:	OK…fine.
MAGGIE:	Ah…
JASON:	Ah-Ma is dead. *(Pause.)*
KARIN:	You're a real bastard! Satisfied!
MAGGIE:	I'm sorry.
JASON:	There. You see how easy that was.
SHU MING:	I don't think…I feel very well.
MAGGIE:	Shu Ming. Are you alright? Oh, you look pale. Come on, we better take you back to the house.

Music: "Snakehead Threat."

Scene 15
Int. Overlapping Voices and Snakehead inside
Shu Ming's Mind

FATHER: Where have you been, Shu Ming?

MAN: We are waiting for good news from you, Shu Ming.

WOMAN: You take care, Shu Ming... Listen to what they say...

SNAKE: You think I won't find you? I'll just turn my back and walk away? What would your father say? How would he feel if he found out I wasn't looking after his only precious child? No, I don't want to do that. Not when your family has sacrificed everything for you. That would be dishonourable. I would never do anything to disappoint my family. Would you? Now, I've been wondering what kind of souvenir I should take back to your father, let him know that you're still thinking of him. I hear Canadian ginseng is out of this world. What about a nice bottle of maple syrup? Or, how about one of your little fingers; or...maybe an ear?

              (*Very serious.*) Don't make it any harder for yourself. It only cheapens you.

                     Music bridge transition, then out.

Scene 16
Int. The Lau's Home

MAGGIE: Are you feeling better?

SHU MING: Yes...thank you. I guess I was just tired.

MAGGIE: It must be the jet lag.

SHU MING: Yes...must be.

MAGGIE: I'm sorry about what happened back at the restaurant. I'm not sure what I was thinking. I never intended to keep it from you. I wanted to tell you before, but you have to understand, there are so many people who still don't know...

SHU MING: I do. I do understand. And I would've done the same.

MAGGIE: Ah-Ma would be so happy to know you finally made it. She would've done anything to get you and your family over.

SHU MING: Yes, we will always be grateful for that. It just wasn't meant to be.

MAGGIE: I'm really glad you're here.

SHU MING: Yes, me too.

MAGGIE: Why don't you stay with us for a while? You can come and work with me, you know, until you find something better. It's nothing to write home about and I can't promise you much, but it might help you get started.

SHU MING: I...

MAGGIE: It's up to you—I don't want to force you or anything.

SHU MING: Everything is happening so fast.

MAGGIE: I think it would be great. And I'm sure the others won't mind...

SHU MING: It's too much to ask...

MAGGIE: Don't be crazy. Old friends shouldn't have to ask. You'll say yes?

SHU MING: Uhh...

MAGGIE: I want you to...

SHU MING: Yes, I'd like that very much.

MAGGIE: Wonderful! You see, it's true: everything old can be new again.

SHU MING: There is something I have to tell you.

MAGGIE: You are not imposing. Don't even think about it...

SHU MING: No...I came here on a boat.

MAGGIE: A boat? What do you mean?

SHU MING: I didn't know how to tell you before. It took me months to get here. I almost didn't make it...I ran away from the Snakehead who arranged to bring me here. I thought I would come to Toronto and work for him, but...I don't know what's happening anymore. Please...I have nowhere else to go.

            Door opening.

KARIN: (*Calling from the back.*) The car's outside. Are you guys coming or not?

MAGGIE: I'm not sure I understand. What is it you expect me to do?

SHU MING: Your mother...I thought maybe—

MAGGIE: It's only us now.

SHU MING: Yes.

KARIN: (*Coming closer.*) Didn't you hear me? (*Beat.*) Shu Ming, what's wrong? Are you OK?

SHU MING: Ah, yes...I think it must be the jet lag.

KARIN: Yes, of course.

MAGGIE: We were just talking about how much there was for us to catch up on.

KARIN: Sure. Well, we'll have lots of time to talk in the car. Are we ready?

MAGGIE: Yes, yes. Let's get going.

Muisc bridge.

Sound of flowing water towards the falls.

Scene 17
Ext. Niagara Falls

The falls. Human activity and gulls overhead, under.

KARIN: Well, what do you think? Isn't it gorgeous?

SHU MING: It's...beautiful. It's even more beautiful than I imagined.

KARIN: See over there? It's New York. That's the American side.

SHU MING: It's so close.

KARIN: Yeah, but the view is so much better here. You see the bridge up there? That's where you can go to cross over. Mom used to love going over to shop at the Mall when it was still the place to be. A trip to Wal-Mart was like going to Disney World. Now, they're everywhere...

JASON: The Wallendas.

KARIN: What?

JASON: The Flying Wallendas. One of the Wallendas brothers did a high-wire walk across the falls over there, maybe twenty-five, thirty years ago.

KARIN: Yeah...I think I saw that on *Biography*. And didn't somebody go over in a barrel too? Isn't that right, Maggie?

MAGGIE: Ah...Evel Knievil.

JASON: What?

KARIN: *Really?*

JASON: Sorry, Maggie. I think that's impossible.

MAGGIE: Houdini, maybe.

KARIN: No, you've got it all mixed up. You're thinking of Marilyn Monroe. She made a movie here.

MAGGIE: I thought she died.

JASON: *(Under.)* Oh, brother...

SHU MING: Did he make it?

KARIN: What's that?

SHU MING: The man...on the wire.

KARIN: The wire? Oh, the wire. You mean the man—

JASON: Yes. *(Silence.)*

KARIN: Well, should we go down and check out the *Maid of the Mist*?

MAGGIE: Ah...maybe that's not such a good idea after all, Karin.

KARIN: What do you mean?

MAGGIE: It's been a long day, we should think about heading back...

KARIN: But, I thought Shu Ming wants to—

MAGGIE: NO! You heard what I said— We're not going!

            Pause.

SHU MING: It's OK, Karin. Your sister's right. I think I've seen enough already. More than I could ever ask for. Thank you so very much.

MAGGIE: Jason, why don't you and I go get the car?

JASON: Uh...sure...whatever. *(Walks away.)*

MAGGIE: You two can wait for us here. We won't be long. *(Walks off.)*

KARIN: I'm sorry. That was so weird. I don't know what got into her. I hope you're not disappointed.

SHU MING: No, not at all.

KARIN: I don't know what her big hurry is. She's been acting strange the whole trip. Did you notice it on the drive down?

SHU MING: I think your sister's tired. She hasn't really stopped since I got here.

KARIN: Still…it's no excuse. *(Silence.)* Look—over there. See the rainbow? You should make a wish…

The falls continue to rage underneath as:

Scene 18
The Falls. Snakehead in Shu Ming's Mind

Music: "Snakehead Theme."

SNAKE: Go ahead…make a wish. What are you afraid of? I must be the furthest thing from your mind. I can't even touch you. You're among friends now. People who love you. They were dying to see you after all these years. Of course they will look after you. Why would they care how you got here? They're immigrants too. Of course they would understand. They've been through it themselves. It's no different. We all have to start somewhere. It's what you do from here on in that matters. So, tell me. What is it that you wished for? I would really like to know…

The falls fade under, cross to:

Music fades out.

Scene 19
Ext. Parking Lot at Niagara Falls

Light road traffic in background, under.

JASON: But she lied to us.

MAGGIE: She was desperate. She had no choice.

JASON: She must've known what she was doing.

MAGGIE: I promised we would help her.

JASON: You don't know what she wants. How can you even trust her?

MAGGIE: I gave her my word. We owe it to Ah-Ma.

JASON: It's not up to us to protect her. We can't carry that burden forever.

MAGGIE: Where is your compassion?

JASON: I'm not the one who broke the law.

MAGGIE: She's like family to us. I know it was a long time ago, Jason. But you remember how close we were. We hated the fact that we had to leave her.

JASON: I can't believe she would do this to us.

MAGGIE: Well, she has. And we are not going to abandon her now.

Sneak "Snakehead Theme" under.

JASON: You're out of your mind. You don't think the Snakehead is going to come looking for her? She owes him.

MAGGIE: We keep it quiet. We don't say anything. Nobody has to know.

JASON: But what about Karin? What if she finds out?

MAGGIE: (*She sighs.*) That's what I need to talk to you about…

                 Sound and music out.

Scene 20
Int. The Lau's Home

KARIN: (*Laughs.*) OK. So listen to this: 'The snake is a seductive creature who protects its loved ones with great care… You are determined to succeed and refuse to be deterred…' Is that true?

SHU MING: I hope you don't judge me by that book.

KARIN: I love reading this stuff…1965. That makes you, 'The Snake Coming Out of the Hole…This Snake is unsure where it is going…you are never quite certain what is happening…your journey—'

SHU MING: Did a white person write that?

KARIN: Why would you say that?

SHU MING: You believe what you want to believe. When you're Chinese, success is more important than anything.

KARIN: So long as you live the life you want to live.

SHU MING: Advantage is everything…

KARIN: I'm not judging you.

SHU MING: I just want a chance.

KARIN: When it comes down to it, isn't that what we all want?

SHU MING: Not everyone is so lucky…

KARIN: You're free to do whatever you want.

SHU MING: I wish that were the case.

KARIN: What do you mean?

SHU MING: I never thought it would come to this.

KARIN: Come to what?

SHU MING: It's not fair. Nobody understands.

KARIN: Tell me. What is it?

SHU MING: My family is counting on me...I can't let them down...

KARIN: It's OK, you haven't done anything wrong.

SHU MING: Karin, about me staying here...

Music transition, cross fade to:

Scene 21
Int. Outside the Lau's Restaurant

Inside quiet dining room, light conversations, electrical cash machines, fish tanks, etc.

Door opening into restaurant.

SNAKE: *(Closing in.)* Excuse me. Are you the owner here?

MAGGIE: Oh...uh...yes, I am.

SNAKE: You know, I was just thinking...this place looks very nice.

MAGGIE: Uh, thank you.

SNAKE: Business going well?

MAGGIE: Uh...yes...just fine.

SNAKE: Good food—

MAGGIE: Pardon me. I'm sorry, but if you're here looking for a job, unfortunately, we're not hiring right now.

SNAKE: Oh, no. You have it all wrong. I don't need a job. I'm actually here looking for my niece. You see, we stopped over for a few days and I seem to have lost her. The thing is, we have to get back on the road tomorrow.

She needs a job. And she has one—waiting for her that is. But I think she wanted to do some sightseeing here and somehow got confused and...well, here I am. Her English isn't very good. Actually, her Chinese is even worse. *(He laughs.)* You know the old saying goes, 'She's one *mahjong* tile short of thirteen.' I'm sure she's just wandering around somewhere. You can't really miss her. She looks like somebody who just got off the boat, if you know what I mean. *(He laughs again.)* She's about this tall. Ah-Ming is her name...Wah Shu Ming.

MAGGIE: Oh...uh...no, actually.

SNAKE: No? Doesn't ring a bell? Well, I'm sure she'll find me before I find her. I guess I'll just have to wait a bit longer. But if by any chance you see her first, could you please let her know I was here? Tell her Big Uncle is getting worried and he's not quite sure what he should do next. Thank you. You are very kind. You have a nice looking restaurant. You must be proud. *(Walking out.)* I'll have to come back and try it sometime soon...

JASON: *(Approaching.)* Maggie...are you alright? Who was that?

MAGGIE: Oh, my god. Where is Shu Ming? We have to get home!

Scene 22
Int. The Lau's Home

MAGGIE: Where is she, Karin?

KARIN: She's gone out for a walk.

JASON: Are you sure?

KARIN: Why would I lie?

JASON: C'mon, this isn't a game.

KARIN: I told you. She's not here.

MAGGIE: Listen carefully, Karin. There's something your brother and I have to tell you.

KARIN: So do I. Shu Ming told me everything.

JASON: What? What did she tell you?

MAGGIE: Karin, Shu Ming is in trouble.

KARIN: I know, she's really scared. We have to help her.

JASON: She's here illegally, Karin! There's nothing we can do to change that.

KARIN: She came here illegally because we discriminate against the poor.

JASON: That doesn't make it right.

KARIN: We are the only family she has here. Why do you think she came to us? She needs our help.

JASON: It's criminal to harbour an illegal alien.

KARIN: She's not a criminal.

JASON: Because you say so? The Snakehead came to the restaurant looking for her. Who did you think got her here? If he finds out we're hiding her...

MAGGIE: Your brother's right, Karin. I was afraid. Maybe the Snakehead already knows she's staying here...

KARIN: If he threatened you, then we should call the police. He has no power over us.

JASON: Have you any idea what he can do to us? Shu Ming belongs to him. He owns her. He was probably taking her to some sweatshop or whorehouse. That's the price you pay to these people.

KARIN: It doesn't have to be that way. There are
             immigration lawyers who can help her. They can
             seek amnesty on humanitarian grounds. We can't
             just give up.

JASON: Well, what then, let them all in? Put out a sign on
             our door, 'Illegals welcome?' See how the
             neighbours feel about that.

KARIN: Who gives a damn what other people think!

JASON: Will you just listen for once?

KARIN: To you? Why? I'm so tired of listening to you. What
             are you going to say to me that you haven't said
             already?

MAGGIE: That's not fair, Karin.

KARIN: Oh, no?

JASON: You think I don't care?

KARIN: You never have, why should it be any different
             now?

MAGGIE: Please…

JASON: You don't even know who I am.

KARIN: Whose fault is that? All you ever do is to criticize.
             You think the whole world is out to get you. But it's
             you. You're the one who chooses to be miserable. So
             don't dump any of that on us here. We don't want it.

JASON: You don't respect a word I say! You want me to
             admit what a terrible brother I've been to you?
             Where were you when Dad died and I had to drop
             everything to keep the restaurant going? What
             sacrifices have you made to deserve my respect?
             You've never had to sweat a day in your life. So
             don't tell me what to do.

MAGGIE: Jason…don't. Maybe we can borrow some money

and pay off the Snakehead. If that's all he wants, maybe we can give it to him.

JASON: What good is that going to do? You always said that Ah-Ma wanted us to keep up a good face. Well, look at us now. *(Beat.)* I was just as happy to see her as either of you—I was. Jesus, if it were anybody else, I'd say sent her back right now. But our life will be ruined if we take her in. People will find out what we've done and we'll be judged all over again. I've spent my whole life working just to try and fit in. I don't need a boat full of freeloaders to come here and jeopardize everything. There are poor and desperate people in this country too, but you don't see any of them borrowing thirty grand to go on a cruise looking for Wonderland.

Door opening in back.

KARIN: She's back. You want to tell her now why you want to walk away? Explain to her how you really feel? Here's your chance, go ahead.

MAGGIE: Can we all talk about this?

SHU MING: *(Enters the room.)* Maggie...Jason. You're home.

JASON: That's right, we are.

MAGGIE: Jason...please.

JASON: No. What she's done is wrong. It's wrong and you know it. Have the guts to say so! Come on, Maggie, don't deny it.

MAGGIE: I...ah...

JASON: Look, I can't stay here if she does.

MAGGIE: Please...

JASON: Fine. You've made your choice.

JASON walks away.

Door opens and then slams shut.

MAGGIE: *(Silence.)* Shu Ming...listen, what Jason said, I'm
              sure he doesn't really mean it...

SHU MING: When I came here on the boat, I kept telling myself I
              would come see you, no matter what...that you
              would be happy to see me, and everything would
              be...alright...we would be all like family
              again...remember?

MAGGIE: I'm so sorry...

SHU MING: 'Only a hundred-thousand yuan for the perfect
              dream,' my father said. A hundred-thousand
              yuan... If I stayed in China and worked at the toy
              factory in the city for the rest of my life I would
              never make that much. The Snakehead told Father if
              I worked hard enough over here, I could maybe
              earn that in a year. He talked about the wonderful
              life I would have, and how proud I would make my
              family... How could you say no to the perfect
              dream?

MAGGIE: You don't have to go. Maybe...maybe there's a way.
              We can help you pay off the Snakehead... Karin
              thinks Immigration would listen...

KARIN: There are no guarantees, but we can try.

SHU MING: And if it doesn't work? What do I say to my family
              when I'm sent back? That they made so many
              sacrifices for me, and all I've brought them is
              shame? Provided the Chinese government doesn't
              throw me in prison first.

MAGGIE: Is that what you think would happen to you?

SHU MING: I'm not exactly welcome anywhere right now.

MAGGIE: That's not true.

SHU MING: You didn't ask for this.

MAGGIE: No. I've never asked for anything. *(Pause.)* Please stay.

SHU MING: And then what...so we can all live a lie? No one forced me to come here. You do what you have to do. Isn't that how we were taught growing up? It's like what Father used to say when he went fishing by the river, 'Even if you know there is no fish in the water, you still throw the net in, because sooner or later...the fish might come back.'

MAGGIE: *(Overlapping.)* '...the fish might come back.' *(Pause.)*

SHU MING: I know at least I'll be doing some good for my family. I'm sure Jason feels he's doing the same. I'm going. I know what I'm doing isn't right for everyone, but it is for me.

MAGGIE: You'll be alright?

SHU MING: Of course.

MAGGIE: I'll see you again?

SHU MING: Yes. *Joy Geen.* (See you.)

            Piano theme bridge to:

Scene 23
Ext. Parents' Grave at the Cemetery

            A few birds. A crisp, calm day.

KARIN: She wanted to be here.

MAGGIE: I know...

KARIN: She's very brave.

MAGGIE: Yes, she is. *(Pause.)* Have you seen your brother?

KARIN: No... Do you want to wait?

MAGGIE: Just a little while longer...those are nice flowers. Mom and Dad are happy.

KARIN: It's their favourite.

MAGGIE: Mine too. (*Silence.*) Karin, I've spent my whole life pretending. I do what others think is right instead of what I believe in my heart. All those years I just watched Ah-Ma and thought, 'She knows. She has a plan. Just follow her.'

KARIN: Mom wasn't perfect.

MAGGIE: She did her best.

KARIN: (*Pause.*) You know, Maggie. When Dad passed away, I was angry more than I was sad. His retirement lasted all of two months—that was it. That was the only time I knew my father didn't work. And it had to take cancer to do it. We watched him slave away at the restaurant day in and day out and we did nothing. I thought we were so selfish. But now, I think maybe that's the way Dad wanted it. He sacrificed everything so we could be just that—live our lives. It's why he came here. And for his reward...it just didn't seem fair.

MAGGIE: It's alright, Karin.

KARIN: And then, when Mom died...it's been tough, you know, this past year. I really miss her.

MAGGIE: You two had a very special relationship, I know. She spoiled you like a jewel.

KARIN: She did...and I didn't deserve it. But, you're right— I admit it.

MAGGIE: You are going to make them both very happy, though...finish school...get a good job...find yourself a nice husband...

KARIN: Uh, yeah...

MAGGIE: You are very lucky, Ah-Mui.

KARIN: I know.

MAGGIE: You don't forget.

KARIN: No, I won't...you too.

JASON: *(Up close.)* I'm here.

                    Music: "Closing Theme."

MAGGIE: Jason.

JASON: Hi, Maggie...Karin...

KARIN: Hey, big brother.

JASON: Uh...I'm sorry I'm late.

MAGGIE: It's alright.

JASON: So, can I light the incense?

MAGGIE: Yes...please do.

                    A match is lit.

                    Music: "Closing Theme."

                    The End.

Entry Denied

Sugith Varughese

Sugith Varughese

Sugith Varughese wrote and directed the first Genie-nominated short film from the prestigious Canadian Film Centre, *Kumar and Mr.* *Jones*, which went on to win several international prizes. He continues to write and direct dramas for television, including *Mela's Lunch,* an award-winning children's drama for the NFB and *On My Mind: The Secret Life of Goldfish* which was nominated for a Gemini and a Writer's Guild of Canada award.

Recent projects include writing a cross-cultural animated anthology series for the National Film Board, called *Talespinners*, which was nominated for a Black Film and Video writing award and won the BFVA best short film award and a Writers Guild of Canada Top Ten Award. His latest short film, *Tongue Tied* premiered at the ReelWorld Film Festival in Toronto.

About the Play

Entry Denied is a period drama about the true events surrounding the arrival of 376 Indian immigrants aboard the *Komagata Maru* in Vancouver in 1914. As British subjects, they had come to challenge an unjust Canadian order-in-council enacted to prevent further immigration from Asia. The story is seen through the eyes of Mewa Singh, a Sikh mill worker who arrived in Canada several years earlier and whose brother, Munshi languishes on the boat as it is kept in the harbour for weeks, with only sporadic food and water brought on board. Mewa tries to obtain special consideration for his brother from William Charles Hopkinson, the immigration official orchestrating efforts to keep the passengers from landing. As events spiral out of control, both men learn the value of dreams against the movement of history and fate.

What follows is a true story. All historical documents quoted are from actual publications. All major characters except Fiona actually existed and the events depicted are historically accurate. However, there is no evidence that Mewa and Munshi were brothers or even knew each other.

Cast

MEWA SINGH: .... Damon D'Oliveira

HOPKINSON: .... Paul Essiembre

REID: .... Peter Donaldson

NARRATOR: .... Maggie Huculak

MUNSHI: .... Sanjay Talwar

FIONA: .... Debra Pollitt

BALWANT SINGH: .... Vik Sahay

BELA SINGH: .... Sugith Varughese

RAHIM: .... Anand Rajaram

GURDIT SINGH: .... Sam Moses

MUNSHI'S WIFE: .... Ranuma Panthaky

HOPKINSON'S SON: .... Josh Buckle

OTHER VOICES: .... David McIlwraith, Les
Carlson, Adrian, Morningstar, Jonathan Whittaker

Production Credits

Producer/Director: .... Damiano Pietropaolo

Associate Producer: .... Colleen Wooods

Original Music: .... Cyrus Sundersingh

Script Editor: .... Dave Carley

Casting: .... Julia Tate

Recording Engineer: .... Wayne Richards

Sound Effects: .... Joe Mahoney

Press Room

Newspaper printing press.

NARRATOR: The *Vancouver Daily Province*, October 15, 1906. The steamship *Empress of Japan* reached port this afternoon from the Orient. She brought in over a hundred Hindus. As soon as the Immigration Inspector examines these men, those who are able to pass will be freed and allowed to go where they will, as any British subject. As noted in Saturday's issue, Mayor Buscombe feels that the community is threatened with great danger by the influx of the East Indians.

Cross fade to: Ext. Vancouver docks

Cold wind blowing. Harbour sounds, sea gulls.

REID: *(Late 30s, coming on.)* Right Hopkinson, who's next?

HOPKINSON: *(30s, Anglo-Indian accent.)* This one, Reid.

REID: Translate for me, Hopkinson. *(To MEWA, slowly as if talking to a deaf man.)* The doctor is going to examine you while you answer our questions.

HOPKINSON: He speaks English.

REID: Indeed. Name?

MEWA: *(20s, shivering.)* Mewa Singh, sahib.

REID writes on his clipboard.

REID: This is Canada. There are no "sahibs" here. My name is Mr. Reid of the Immigration Department. You'd do well to remember it. Place of birth?

MEWA: Gulpur. Mr. Reid. Sir.

DOCTOR: Open your mouth. Say "ah."

MEWA: Ah...

HOPKINSON: That's in Jullundar district, isn't it? Is the bird sanctuary still there?

MEWA: *(Surprised at his knowledge.)* I have heard of it, but I could never go.

HOPKINSON: Of course not. But there are no such restrictions in this country.

REID: Right. Well Hopkinson? In your expert opinion, is this one going to be trouble?

HOPKINSON: No, I have no reason to suspect him of disloyalty to the empire. Do I, Mewa Singh?

MEWA: It is because of the empire that I could even come.

HOPKINSON: *(Laughing.)* Very true.

REID: Cheeky bugger.

DOCTOR: He appears to be clean, Mr. Reid.

REID: Pity. *(Moving off.)* Right, what's your name? *(Wild line in background.:* Why do all you people have the same last name?*)*

           REID examines next passenger in background.

HOPKINSON: Excellent. By the way, my name's Hopkinson. We immigration chaps aren't all like Mr. Reid there. Sat Sri Akal.

MEWA: *(Pleasantly surprised.)* Sat Sri Akal.

HOPKINSON: You'll be wanting a job, I expect.

MEWA: I will find one.

HOPKINSON: There's a mill owner in Kitsilano who's been hiring a lot of your chaps. His name's Webster. Mention my name, if you like.

MEWA: *(Moving off.)* Thank you, Mr. Hopkinson.

HOPKINSON: Good luck, Mewa Singh. And welcome to Canada.

Ext. Sawmill

Sawmill ambience in background.

WEBSTER: *(Coming on.)* So Hopkinson sent you, eh?

MEWA: *(Coming on.)* I can work hard, Mr. Webster.

WEBSTER: Hindoos get a dollar a day.

MEWA: But mill work is TWO dollars a day.

WEBSTER: *(Laughs.)* That's what I'd have to pay a white man. It's up to you.

White workers milling about the gate.

LUMBER
WORKER: *(Off.)* Mr. Webster!

WEBSTER: Frank. What're you boys doing here?

LUMBER
WORKER: We'd like to know when you're taking us back on, sir.

WEBSTER: Depends. *(To MEWA.)* Well, do you want the job?

MEWA: Yes.

WEBSTER: *(To lumber workers.)* Sorry lads, I have all the workers I need.

The workers groan and mutter angrily among themselves.

LUMBER
WORKER: Those bloody Hindoos are taking our jobs, Mr. Webster!

WEBSTER: Don't blame me. I'm just running a business.

Mill whistle blows to end the shift.

Music: under...

MEWA's first letter.

MEWA: *(V.O.)* "Vancouver, December 25th. My dearest brother, Munshi. Today the mill is closed for the Christmas. I still cannot believe it is me instead of you who came here. When the ticket agent in Calcutta said the fare had doubled...

Ext. Calcutta backstreets.

Street sounds: Chaiwallahs, paanwallahs, rickshaws, and the occasional motorized vehicle sputtering past.

MEWA: No, no, no. You must go, Munshi. You are my elder brother.

MUNSHI: Tsch. This was your idea from the start. If you make money, then send for me.

MEWA: What will they say back home in Gulpur, if you stay and I go?

MUNSHI: That one of us was brave and one of us was smart.

MEWA: It would not be right.

MUNSHI: Then let fate decide. Give me an anna.

MEWA: Fate brings nothing but trouble.

MUNSHI: The money you spent on that ticket is half mine.

MEWA: *(Sighs.)* Heads.

A coin being flipped. It falls on the cobblestones.

MUNSHI: *(Disappointed.)* Tails.

MEWA: *(Stoutly.)* The ticket is yours, Munshi. Now, we must find the Calcutta gurdwara and in the morning, I will see you off...

MUNSHI: You should have won.

MEWA: *(Warmly.)* Fate is fate...

            MEWA'S first letter.

            (V.O.) You won, Munshi, but you did not trust fate. When I woke up, you were gone and the ticket was beside me. That is the lesson you have taught me. Don't give in to fate. So I have enclosed the first payment towards my debt to you. Some day soon, I will be at the Vancouver docks to welcome you.

            Music out.

            Ext. MEWA's shack.

            In the distance, a dog barks.

            Clothes being washed in a large tub.

BALWANT
SINGH: *(30s, intense.)* *(Off.)* Washing clothes is woman's work.

MEWA: When they allow our women into this country, I will let them do it.

BALWANT
SINGH: *(Coming on.)* My name is Balwant Singh.

MEWA: I have heard of you. I am not interested in joining your fight.

BALWANT
SINGH: It is not just my fight. We are servants in our own country and in every other country of the Empire. That is what it means for us to be British subjects.

MEWA: I agree with you. But after you are all dead, what then?

BALWANT
SINGH: It is because we are willing to die that we will have
                independence in India. What are you willing to do?

MEWA: My death will only hurt my mother. I want to fight,
                but with money, not bullets. I will go to business
                school and learn bookkeeping.

BALWANT
SINGH: Bookkeeping! Now that is woman's work.

MEWA: A rich Indian is more dangerous to the British than a
                dead one.

                Int. School corridor

                Working-class women entering a classroom.

FIONA: *(Mid 20s.)* Just take any desk. Good evening. Hello…
                Er, can I help you?

MEWA: *(Coming on.)* Room twelve? Adult bookkeeping?

FIONA: That's correct.

MEWA: I want to enroll, please.

                The women stop talking, some whisper in alarm.

FIONA: I see. Did you know there's a five dollar fee?

MEWA: Here it is.

FIONA: Perhaps you didn't know, but there are usually just
                women in the class. It's a course for women.

MEWA: I don't mind.

FIONA: Well, you're a very modern thinker.

MEWA: Schooling is very ancient thinking for my people.

FIONA: Right then. Your name?

MEWA: Mewa Singh. M…e…w…

WOMAN: *(Coming on.)* I've changed my mind. I'd like my money back, if you please.

FIONA: Oh—well, as this gentleman is enrolling, I just happen to have it.

WOMAN: You don't have another banknote?

FIONA: What's wrong with it?

The woman walks away.

FIONA: Right, class. Let's begin. Please open your books to page 3, the chapter titled "Record Keeping."

Cross fade to:

Int. Church basement

A blast from a Scout whistle.

REID: Patrol formation! Hurry up!

A troop of boys scurry into position.

REID: Evening, Hopkinson. What have we here?

HOPKINSON: My son would like to become a Boy Scout.

REID: Would he? Excellent. *(To HOPKINSON's son.)* So, you're here to join the Scouts, eh lad?

HOPKINSON's
SON: *(Age 10.)* Yes, sir.

REID: Well, anyone can join, but only a few reach the top. Do you want to give it a try?

HOPKINSON: Of course he does. Right, Simon?

REID: Well, join the back of that line, lad.

HOPKINSON's
SON: *(Moving off.)* Yes, sir.

The troop is getting rambunctious.

Several blasts from the whistle to quiet them.

REID: Boys. Ah, we'll make a Scout of him, Hopkinson. *(Moving off.)* If he's willing.

HOPKINSON: *(Calling.)* It's what he wants.

REID blows his whistle—

Cross fade to: Int. MEWA'S shack.

Music under…

Snores of several men sleeping.

In the distance, the dog barks.

Suddenly, a rock crashes through a window. Glass breaking, the rock lands on the wooden floor.

Men leap up. Shouts in Punjabi.

MEWA: Look! Outside! The next shack is on fire!

NARRATOR: …to place on record an emphatic protest against the proposed introduction into this Province of Hindoo labourers, and call on the workingmen of British Columbia to assist by every means in their power, in preventing this further attempt to flood the country with cheap Asiatic labour. The Trades and Labour Councils of Vancouver and Victoria, August 3, 1906.

From outside, a well-liquored mob smashing everything in sight.

LUMBER
WORKER: *(Off.)* Damn Hindoos! Teach the wogs a lesson, boys!

MEWA: RUN!

The men stampede for the door.

Ugly, violent sounds as the Indians try to fight off their attackers.

Fade out.

Int. Classroom.

FIONA walks up and down the rows.

FIONA: *(Off, coming closer.)* Thank you…thank you. I'll have these corrected for your next class.

Footsteps stop.

FIONA: Your assignment, Mewa?

MEWA: I do not have it.

Murmurs of disapproval from the other students.

FIONA: I see. Well, bring it next time, then.

MEWA: I will not be able to then, either Miss.

Even more shock from the women.

FIONA: Why not?

MEWA: *(Burning with shame.)* I no longer have a text book.

A few tongue-clucks from the other women.

MEWA: It is not my fault! It was burned.

FIONA: Ah, I heard there was a fire in the Indian colony.

MEWA: They burned it. They burned everything. They destroyed our home! It meant nothing to them.

FIONA: I'm sorry. Well, I'm sure the police will find the ruffians who did it. Meanwhile, you need a text book. You can borrow mine.

Book placed on desk.

Whispers of surprise and even shock from the women.

MEWA: Thank you, Miss Fiona. I will take excellent care of it, I promise you.

FIONA: *(Moving off.)* Right. Now that we all have textbooks, let's open them to page twenty-three.

Cross-fade to Press Room

                Newspaper printing press.

NARRATOR: *The Globe and Mail,* January 8, 1908. The Department of the Interior has under consideration a new departure in regard to immigration. The intention is to amend the regulations so that in future all immigrants must come direct to Canada from their place of birth or the country of citizenship. While it is not framed against any particular class of immigrants it will have the effect of shutting out Japanese and Indians coming from Honolulu to British Columbia.

                Int. Solicitor's office.

                Quiet tick-tock of a clock.

SOLICITOR: I'm a lawyer, not a politician. I'm not sure what I can do for you.

MEWA: I want you to take my case.

                Paper shuffling. Pages of a book being flipped.

SOLICITOR: The orders-in-council are very specific. All immigrants must now arrive in Canada by continuous passage.

MEWA: But there are no steamship lines which give continuous passage from India.

SOLICITOR: I suspect the government knew that.

MEWA: So you must petition the government on my behalf! Say I will be Munshi's sponsor and guardian. He would never become a destitute.

                Book being shut.

SOLICITOR: Writing letters to the Minister would be a waste of time and expense. I can't, in good conscience, take your case. It wouldn't be right to take your money.

Leather chair creaks. Footsteps.

SOLICITOR: Now, if you'll excuse me.

Door opens.

MEWA: Then can you recommend a lawyer who is willing to take my money?

SOLICITOR: I'm afraid not. No one can help you. You have no case.

The door shuts.

Music sting.

Int. Kitchen.

Steam bursts out of a kettle with a high-pitched whistle. The burner is shut off.

The door bursts open.

REID: *(Coming on.)* Cable from the British Consulate in Hong Kong! Would you believe a boatload of Indians have chartered an old Japanese coal scow—

HOPKINSON: The *Komagata Maru.*

REID: *(A beat, then.)* Bound for Vancouver—

HOPKINSON: They should set sail in three weeks.

REID: See here, Hopkinson, they are going to challenge the law by chartering this damn boat to bring them here.

HOPKINSON: It's a shrewd effort.

REID: Shrewd, is it! Pah, I have no time for gamesmanship with these Hindoos.

HOPKINSON: Most of the passengers are Sikhs. Different religion from Hindu.

REID: Whatever they are, it's my job to keep them out. And yours, too. Or don't you remember? And what are those letters?

HOPKINSON: What would you say is the most powerful weapon of the twentieth century?

REID: What? Um, the tank? No—the battleship!

HOPKINSON: I don't think so. Information. Information will give power in the modern age. These letters are the Indian colony's mails. They rest with me awhile before continuing on their way.

A knock on the open door.

CLERK: *(Off.)* Mr. Hopkinson? *(Coming on.)* There's a note for you from a solicitor, a Mr. William Hall.

The clerk leaves.

Envelope being torn open.

HOPKINSON: That's what I traffic in, Reid. Information. *(He reads.)*

REID: What is it?

HOPKINSON: Nothing. Nothing that concerns you.

Music under.

Int. Gurdwara.

GRANTHI and musicians sing a hymn accompanying themselves on drum and harmonium.

BELA: *(30's, genial.) (Coming on.)* Prayer is the last resort of a desperate man.

MEWA: Who says I am desperate?

BELA: You are praying. Prayers and lawyers can't help you, Mewa Singh.

MEWA: Who are you?

BELA: My name is Bela Singh. *(Conspiratorially.)* I am a spy!

MEWA: Leave me alone.

BELA: I can be your magic helper. All you have to do is ask.

MEWA: What do you want?

BELA: Maybe your prayers have been answered.

MEWA: How?

BELA: Come with me and find out.

> *Music out.*
>
> *Dissolve to: Int. HOPKINSON's office.*
>
> *A knock.*

HOPKINSON: Come!

> *Door opens.*

BELA: I have returned, Mr. Hopkinson. With Mewa Singh.

HOPKINSON: Good. You remember me? From the docks?

> *Pen dropped on blotter.*

MEWA: Yes. He said you could help me.

HOPKINSON: Did you say that, Bela Singh?

BELA: I told him you would answer his prayers.

HOPKINSON: Tsch. So you went to see a lawyer, Mewa.

MEWA: How did...? Yes, but he didn't take my case.

> *A fountain pen writing on paper.*

HOPKINSON: If he had, you would have brought a great deal of trouble on yourself, I fear.

MEWA: No Canadian lawyer is going to let me get into trouble, Mr. Hopkinson.

             HOPKINSON caps the pen and puts it down.

HOPKINSON: Well, I don't know about answering your prayers but there's a boat been chartered to bring Indians here by continuous passage and challenge the law.

MEWA: Everyone has heard of it. And everyone knows they will not be allowed entry.

HOPKINSON: Mmm…not all. But one man, perhaps. If that man has a friend. Who himself has a friend.

MEWA: For the friendship of a man like you what could I possibly offer in exchange?

HOPKINSON: That is not how friendship works. You don't owe me anything. Nothing at all.

             Int. Telegraph office.

             Morse code beeping.

MEWA: *(V.O.)* "Munshi Singh, Gulpur, Jullundar District, the Punjab. Book passage on *Komagata Maru* bound for Vancouver, stop. Have made arrangements for your entry, regardless of boat's fate, stop. Mewa."

             Dissolve to: Int. Classrooom.

             A soft knock.

             Miss Fiona?

FIONA: Oh, hello. It's not your night, is it?

MEWA: I came to tell you that I cannot attend tomorrow night's class. Here is my assignment.

             He hands her some papers.

FIONA: Oh. Alright.

MEWA: I would not miss for any reason, except that my brother arrives tomorrow.

FIONA: Oh, I see. But I thought they were no longer allowing any more immigrants from India.

MEWA: Only those who cannot come by a direct passage. My brother is on a boat chartered to come directly from India. They will have fulfilled the government's rule.

FIONA: Well that's rather ingenious. If we left things up to the powers that be, nothing would ever change.

MEWA: You understand. I will see you in two weeks, then. Perhaps I will convince my brother to enroll in your class.

FIONA: If he's as committed as you, it will be a pleasure to have him.

Ext. Immigration launch.

The immigration launch cutting through water.

REID: They'll save themselves a lot of trouble, if they just agree to turn the *Komagata Maru* around and go right back to the Poonjab.

HOPKINSON: They're British subjects, Reid. They're entitled to due process.

REID: Look at them, lined up on the deck.

HOPKINSON: The Muslims are wearing the red caps. The rest look like Hindus and Sikhs. The turbaned are Sikhs. Look, those ones are wearing khaki.

REID: What religion are they?

HOPKINSON: They served in the British army.

Music sting.

Ext. Komagata Maru.

Footsteps on wooden deck approach.

HOPKINSON: *(Coming on.)* You would be Gurdit Singh. Sat Sri Akal.

GURDIT
SINGH: *(50s.)* Sat Sri Akal. Mr. Hopkinson, I presume?

REID: How does he know your name?

GURDIT
SINGH: The Inspector is well known to us Indians.

HOPKINSON: This is my colleague, Mr. Malcolm Reid. And who's this?

GURDIT
SINGH: My son. He is ten. He would like to live in Canada. As would we all.

HOPKINSON: I have a son about his age.

GURDIT
SINGH: Perhaps they would like to play together.

HOPKINSON: I'm sure. But I don't think that will happen, Mr. Singh.

REID: Ha! I can guarantee it won't!

GURDIT
SINGH: We have complied with your laws.

REID: Well, you're not coming ashore today.

GURDIT
SINGH: We are British citizens and we consider we have a right to enter any part of the Empire! We are determined to make this a test case and if we are refused entrance into your country, the matter will not end here!

Disslove to: Int. Dominion Hall

Theatre ambience: A crowd o five huundred, tense and angry.

RAHIM: *(Addressing the crowd from the stage.)* The exclusion law of this white dominion is but the latest tyranny against Indians in the Empire. Nowhere do we have a home—not even in India!

              Fervent applause.

              Three times Sikh warriors fought against the British. It is time once again. We need weapons. But this time our weapons are not swords and bullets, but money to fight for the lives of our brothers on the boat. Money to send a message to the British. Indians never, never, never shall be slaves!

              Cheers and wild applause surges from the audience.

MEWA: Mr. Rahim! Mr. Rahim!—

AUDIENCE: *(Quiets.)*

MEWA: My brother is on the boat! Do you know—

AUDIENCE: I have a cousin!/My sister-in-law's nephew—/ What about my son!

RAHIM: This meeting was called for business, not talk!

              Audience quiets again.

              The passengers need food and water. We need to pay the charter for the boat, otherwise the owners will demand the boat return to Hong Kong—even if the passengers are not landed. Mr. Reid knows this. That is why he does nothing! What our Shore Committee needs is hard cash. Enough to keep the boat in Vancouver whatever they try and do.

              Applause.

              Dissolve to: Int. Dominion Hall

              Hands expertly counting wads of cash.

MEWA: *(Coming on.)* My brother is on the boat, Mr. Rahim. His name is Munshi Singh.

RAHIM: *(After checking the passenger manifest.)* Yes, there is a Munshi Singh. From Gulpur?

MEWA: What are the legal actions your Shore Committee will take?

RAHIM: Gurdit Singh has hired a lawyer and we will pay.

MEWA: Who will be the test case to see who qualifies for entry under the law?

RAHIM: There will be no test case. Mr. Reid will not let that happen.

MEWA: My brother would qualify and then they would all get in!

RAHIM: The longer we can keep that boat in the harbour, the better their chances of entry. If you want to help your brother, be on the docks tomorrow. We can use an extra pair of hands.

Music bridge…

Int. Dominion Hall.

Audience, tense murmurs.

As chairman of the Shore Committee, I want to thank our lawyer, Mr. J. Edward Bird for coming and to ask him for a report on his progress.

Chair scraping as BIRD stands.

BIRD: Now I'm not here as a politician. I am in this matter simply as a lawyer and I have tried to the best of my ability to get a test case before the courts for the purpose of finding out as to whether these men are entitled to land or not. Why I have not been able to do this, gentlemen, I cannot say. The government talks about socialists and anarchists. There is no set of anarchists in Canada like the Immigration Officials who defy all law and order. I can see some of the Immigration Officials right here, so I tell you, do not blame the Hindus if you see this farce dragged on for months. If necessary they can wait a century—perhaps they will all die before this thing is decided.

Loud applause.

Int. MAYOR T.S. BAXTER's office.

MAYOR
BAXTER: But that boat's been sitting there for weeks. Can't they be confined in a detention shed on the wharf? It makes the city look bad, that boat sitting in the harbour for all to see.

REID: Mr. Mayor, the one thing I'm worried about is a riot.

               Councilmen reacting with harumphed alarm.

MAYOR
BAXTER: Well, I've heard these blasted Hindoos are a volatile race.

REID: I meant our own folk. Best keep a mile of water separating the combatants. Now there are even Hindoos protesting on the docks every day. Probably sending signals to the boat by some secret semaphore, for all we know.

MAYOR
BAXTER: What we have to fear the most is not the Hindoos now here, but the millions that are going to arrive unless we stop them.

COUNCILMEN: *(Agree.)* "Hear hear!"

REID: Then let our deportation procedure run its course. I've already denied them entry.

MAYOR
BAXTER: Then why aren't they gone?

REID: Well, they have a right to an appeal.

MAYOR
BAXTER: Each one of 'em? That will take months!

REID: Don't you see? They'll give up long before.

HOPKINSON: They need fresh water, Mayor Baxter. Some food.

REID: What are you saying, Hopkinson? Then they could hold out forever!

HOPKINSON: Think what the newspapers would say if one of them died, Mr. Mayor.

REID: It would be hidden on page six next to the tide reports.

MAYOR
BAXTER: I'm cabling the Prime Minister. Their right to appeal needs to be curtailed. And get some fresh water to that boat.

Dissolve to: Ext. Waterfront.

Harbour sounds, gulls.

The Indians playing a casual game of cricket. Crack! as the batsman hits the ball. Applause. Continue under...

BALWANT
SINGH: This cricket game is how you protest?

MEWA: We are just playing, Balwant. It passes the time.

BALWANT
SINGH: Look at that boat, baking in the harbour. Four weeks it has been. *(Snorts.)* They actually thought they would be allowed to land?

MEWA: They came to challenge an unjust law.

BALWANT
SINGH: And you think your protest will make one bit of difference to the authorities?

MEWA: At least the people of this city know what we want. What could you do to get them off?

BALWANT
SINGH: Getting them off? You really don't understand, do you? But I will not just let them rot. They can still help the cause.

MEWA: *(Alarmed.)* Balwant! What are you going to do?

BALWANT
SINGH: Go back to your boy's game. *(Moving off.)* Come to me when you are ready to be a man.

> *Ext. The sawmill.*
>
> *Sawmill working in background. Under...*
>
> *Thud! As MEWA stacks boards.*
>
> *Feet on gravel approaching.*

HOPKINSON: *(Coming on.)* Afternoon, Mewa.

MEWA: Mr. Hopkinson.

HOPKINSON: Bela Singh said you had some information.

> *Thud! MEWA resumes his work.*

MEWA: *(Urgently.)* You must see that they are granted entry, before it's too late.

HOPKINSON: What do you know, Mewa?

MEWA: I don't know anything. But I fear... it's Balwant Singh. I think he has dangerous plans for the boat.

HOPKINSON: I'm not surprised. He needs martyrs.

MEWA: He will have them unless they are allowed to land.

HOPKINSON: Actually, it's not the government that's stopping them. It's Rahim.

MEWA: What has he done?

HOPKINSON: Well, as head of the Shore Committee, he needs to be convinced of the merit of a test case—one passenger to represent all passengers—to see if Reid was within his rights to deny them entry. Perhaps you can convince "Mr. Rahim" to cooperate, and I can get your brother off the boat in the doing.

MEWA: Rahim won't listen to me.

HOPKINSON: Because he is a Hindu?

MEWA: Because he is a businessman.

Bridge to next scene.

HOPKINSON: What if I could give you a means of persuasion?

Int. RAHIM's office.

A door opens and shuts.

RAHIM: Mewa. What are you doing here?

MEWA: *(Coming on.)* I am here to speak to Mr. Varma.

RAHIM: *(Taken aback, then.)* There is no Varma here.

MEWA: Oh, I think Mr. Varma is here. And I think I am speaking to him. And I also think that Mr. Jamshedji Nanporia of Kobe, Japan would be happy to know of his whereabouts also. You have some accounts to settle with him?

RAHIM: *(Thinks, then.)* Shut the door. What do you want?

MEWA: My brother is on the boat. I want you to agree to make him the test case.

RAHIM: Out of the question.

MEWA: They are starving! It is their only hope.

RAHIM: You are a fool! This is just what the government wants.

MEWA: No. This is what I want.

Dissolve to: Int. City Jail.

Footsteps on stone approaching.

Metal jail door unlocks and creaks open.

HOPKINSON: Just a few minutes, Mewa.

MEWA: *(Breathless.)* They let me bring you your food.

MUNSHI: Mewa!

Music under...

A metal tray being placed down.

They embrace.

MEWA: Munshi...

Bedsprings squeak.

MUNSHI: Oh... I can't stand.

MEWA: You must eat, Munshi. Eat, eat!

MUNSHI begins to eat. Ravenous.

MUNSHI: *(Chewing.)* Living in Canada has made you fat. You should spend some time on the boat.

MEWA: *(A soft laugh, then intense.)* I would give anything to take your place.

MUNSHI: So would I. *(Beat, then chuckles.)*

Music out.

MEWA: I don't know why things have happened like this.

MUNSHI: It is just fate.

MEWA: Fate did not bring you here! I did.

MUNSHI: *(Chuckling.)* You finally fulfilled one of your boasts.

MEWA: You are almost free, Munshi. You are the test case. I arranged it.

MUNSHI reaches into his pocket and gives MEWA an envelope.

MUNSHI: Will you mail this? It's to my wife.

MEWA: Your wife! You never wrote me…

MUNSHI: We married just before we sailed.

MEWA: Tell me about her. She must be beautiful.

MUNSHI: She is. Her name is Jaswinder. She will worry when news gets to India about the boat.

MEWA: Jaswinder. Munshi… no matter what happens, you will be free. I have a friend—

HOPKINSON: *(Coming on.)* Right Mewa, time's up.

MEWA: Five minutes more, Mr. Hopkinson. Please—

HOPKINSON: You musn't push your luck, Mewa Singh. And you've been given more than any Indian in the colony.

Footsteps on stone moving away.

MEWA: *(Moving off.)* I will mail it in tomorrow's post, Munshi. I promise!

MUNSHI: Mewa!

Door clangs shut. And locks.

Footsteps moving away, echoing.

Press Room

Newspaper printing press.

NARRATOR: *(V.O. Court proceedings.) Vancouver Daily Province,* June 29, 1914. The Hindu case reached the British Columbia Court of Appeal today. The court sitting today consisted of their lordships Chief Justice MacDonald, Justices Irving, Martin, McPhillips and

Gallagher. In court were half a dozen Hindus, all wearing their turbans. They stood, stalwart and stolid, six-footers all of them, when the court crier announced the coming of their lordships. The case today was entitled In re: Munshi Singh. That gentleman was not present however. He is still enjoying himself in custody.

> *Int. Main court room, B.C. Court of Appeal, Victoria.*

BIRD:

Therefore, Canada does not have the right to exclude British subjects because the British-North America Act, which created Canada, did not give her that power.

JUSTICE
MARTIN:

Mr. Bird, could we not keep out murderers?

BIRD:

Murderers, your worship?

> *A massive volume being opened, pages flipped.*

JUSTICE
MARTIN:

Section three of the Act clearly prohibits the insane, diseased, crippled, criminal and vagrant. Canada could refuse entry to these people even if they were British subjects.

BIRD:

Uh, well yes...

JUSTICE
GALLIGHER:

Indeed. And, if one class of British subjects could be denied entry, why not another?

BIRD:

My client isn't diseased or crippled or a murderer... he is a farmer!

JUSTICE
IRVING:

Nevertheless, the Act does empower Mr. Reid as an agent of the government the right to issue a deportation order.

BIRD: With all due respect, your lordships... A deportation order deprives my client of his civil rights! The Act authorizing such deportations is... is ultra vires!

JUSTICE
MacDONALD: Mr. Bird, it is the prerogative of this court to declare the law, not to make it.

A gavel slams!

Music...under.

Dissolve to: MEWA's second letter.

MEWA: (V.O.) Vancouver, June 30th. My dearest brother, Today was to be our day of reunion. Instead, I watched them put you on that boat again. When I saw you in the jail, you said it was fate that made this happen. But it wasn't fate. It was laws. That is what they use in Canada to get what they want. They cause pain without spilling a drop of blood. They don't understand fate. But we are Sikhs. Our tenth guru made us warriors. I cannot write more for I do not know who will read this before you. If you are reading this, then you have returned to Gulpur safely. Or I am dead.

Music out.

Int. BALWANT SINGH's rooms.

A knock on the door. It opens.

BALWANT
SINGH: Ah, Hopkinson's man.

MEWA: (*Coming on.*) I do not work for Hopkinson, Balwant Singh.

BALWANT
SINGH: Why was your brother chosen to be the test case, then?

MEWA: It was fate.

BALWANT
SINGH: Why do you come to see me?

MEWA: I see now that you were right.

BALWANT
SINGH: But being right is not enough to help them.

                   Hands shuffling a wad of money.

MEWA: Then will this be enough?

BALWANT
SINGH: It's a lot of money. It will be put to good use.

MEWA: How can I be sure this will be used to help those on
                   the boat directly?

BALWANT
SINGH: You do not trust me?

MEWA: It is not enough for me to just give money.

BALWANT
SINGH: Then, join us. We cross the border tomorrow.

                   Ext. Komagata Maru.

HOPKINSON: Mr. Singh, I have here the necessary papers from the
                   Department of Immigration ordering the
                   deportation. You have been instructed to weigh
                   anchor and leave immediately.

                   Flipping through papers.

GURDIT
SINGH: You actually expect us to leave just like that,
                   Hopkinson?

HOPKINSON: I know what you are getting at and there will be
                   provisions for you once you reach the three mile
                   limit.

GURDIT
SINGH: We need supplies to last all the way to Calcutta. Do
                I have your assurance there will be enough?

HOPKINSON: *(Moving off.)* I'll do what I can.

                HOPKINSON starts to climb down the gangplank.

GURDIT
SINGH: Mr. Hopkinson! We will not leave without your
                word!

HOPKINSON: *(Off, calling back.)* Take my advice Mr. Singh and go
                on your own. Don't make any more trouble.
                Otherwise they'll have to use force.

                Int. Immigration office.

                Office ambience. Telephone ringing in background.

REID: Tell them if they don't leave by six P.M., to hell with
                any provisions.

HOPKINSON: Reid—

REID: By the way Hopkinson, about your son's enrollment
                in the Scouts. I got tired waiting for you to provide
                them, so I wrote to the Yorkshire registrar for your
                birth records.

                Door opens in background. Footsteps approach.

HOPKINSON: I...I would have—

REID: They don't seem to know you.

HOPKINSON: I'm sure it's a mistake.

REID: Well, correct it. Your son can't join without proper
                documentation.

CHIEF
OF POLICE: *(Coming on.)* I thought you gentlemen would want
                to hear this from me personally.

REID: What is it, Chief?

HOPKINSON: The Mounties arrested a Hindoo from the colony
                 trying to sneak back into the province at the Sumas
                 crossing. He was carrying guns. There were others.
                 But they got away.

REID: WHAT! Those sammy bastards weren't content to
                 lose in court, were they! Can't trust 'em. Can't trust
                 the lot of 'em! Right. We are going to board the
                 Komagata Maru with as much force as we can muster
                 while there is still light. How many men can you
                 give me, chief?

CHIEF
OF POLICE: Ten.

REID: Ten!

CHIEF
OF POLICE: That's all I have to spare.

REID: Look chief, there are a good three hundred and fifty
                 crazed Hindoos on that boat and you expect me to
                 rout them with a blessed ten men?

CHIEF
OF POLICE: Well, if you want to wait until one in the morning,
                 then at least the boys'll be finishing their shift. But
                 it'll be time and a half then.

REID: One AM., then. But I want a hundred men, at least!

HOPKINSON: Taking the ship—and at night? News of this will
                 start riots throughout the Empire!

REID: I'm sure the British army can handle a few hot-
                 headed wogs, Hopkinson.

HOPKINSON: Reid—

REID: I've taken it under advisement!

HOPKINSON: And your response will be duly noted in my report.

REID: *(Moving off.)* Now chief, how many rifles can we find for my men?

                 Slam Cut to: Int. MEWA's cell.

                 Clang as the doors open and shut in the corridor.

                 Footsteps on stone as someone approaches. Stops.

HOPKINSON: Have they fed you, Mewa?

MEWA: Yes, Mr. Hopkinson.

HOPKINSON: No mistreatment?

MEWA: No.

HOPKINSON: Good. You will be charged with evading customs with a .32 caliber pistol in your possession. The penalty on conviction is ten years in prison. Cooperate and I can reduce your charge to carrying a concealed weapon. The fine is fifty dollars.

MEWA: No.

HOPKINSON: I don't have the time, Mewa! Just give me their names. *(Silence.)* They are the ringleaders. Why should you be in jail?

MEWA: I just wanted to make sure they didn't get the guns on the boat and turn the passengers into martyrs for their cause.

HOPKINSON: But they will be martyrs, Mewa Singh. Reid is going to storm the boat. I can stop him if I can deliver up the other gun-runners. *(Silence.)* Fine. *(Moving off.)* It will be on your conscience.

                 Footsteps receding.

                 Distant door clangs shut.

                 Ext. Docks.

                 Wooden crate being opened with crowbar.

REID: Let's see what the Hindoos have to say to thirty-five special Immigration Police armed with these new Ross rifles!

CHIEF
OF POLICE: *(Coming on.)* Reid! What the hell are you doing? My men are under orders to check their weapons.

REID: And I'm sure we won't be needing these, chief, but better safe than sorry.

CHIEF
OF POLICE: Let's get on with it, Reid. My men have been on duty all day.

The tug toots its whistle.

Ext. Sea Lion.

Tug's engine trolling.

REID: Someone shine that searchlight onto their deck.

Passengers off, a mighty roar.

HOPKINSON: Look! It's the passengers. It looks like they've got clubs in their hands.

REID: Send over the grappling hook. We'll tow it out to sea!

Tug's grappling hook clangs against the deck of Komagata Maru.

Turn on the pumps!

The tugboat's pumps rumble to life.

Fade the rest of this scene under narrator's voice...

Aim the fire hose right at 'em, Chief!

Water erupting out of the fire hose.

PASSENGERS cry out as they are knocked back by the eruption of cold water.

REID: Prepare to board!

              The tugboat's pumps die.

              Off, a great cry of victory. Fading.

              Int. Immigration office.

              Telegraph beeps.

NARRATOR: *(V.O.)* Prime Minister Robert Borden, Ottawa:
              Hindus on ship apparently desperately
              revolutionary and determined to defy law. Stop.
              Absolutely necessary that strong stand be taken and
              would urge that Naval Department be detailed to
              enforce the situation! Stop. Signed, H.H.Stevens,
              Member of Parliament.

              Dissolve to: Int. MEWA's cell.

              Music...under.

              Feet on stone, pacing.

MEWA: *(Gasps.)* Who's there?... Bela! How did you get in
              here?

BELA: *(Unreal.)* I go where I want.

MEWA: Because you work for Hopkinson.

BELA: Mm. There is a Hopkinson everywhere I go. His
              name may have been different. Different voice,
              different body. But they all have the same eyes. I
              will tell you something, Mewa Singh. Once you find
              the man with those eyes, you can have anything you
              want. What do you want?

MEWA: Nothing.

BELA: Nothing? You are happy in this cell? Isn't there
              anything you want? A secret desire. A hope? A
              dream?

MEWA: I don't have any more dreams.

BELA: Dreams are just shadows until they come true. Then
                they become hard. And real. And flesh and blood.
                Like her.

MEWA: What are you saying?

BELA: Desire is not enough, Mewa Singh. You must learn
                how the world works.

                Feet scraping on stone.

MEWA: Bela? Where—where are you? Are you there? Bela!

Cross Fade to: Press Room

                Newspaper printing press.

NARRATOR: *Vancouver Province,* July 21, 1914. The naval cruiser
                Rainbow arrived in the harbour today, anchoring a
                few hundred yards south-west of the vessel
                Komagata Maru, with 354 Hindoo passengers on
                board, refusing to return peacefully to their
                homeland. In addition to the *Rainbow*'s twelve
                heavy-calibre guns and several machine guns
                aimed at the vessel, a military contingent lined up
                just south of Pier A. There were all in all 204 men in
                uniform. The men presented a very smart
                appearance.

                Ext. Docks.

                *Carnival-on-the-docks atmosphere among the crowd
                gathered on shore. A brass band plays.*

BURRELL: *(Off.)* Where's Reid? *(Now shouting to be heard.)*
                (Coming on.) I said, which one's Reid?!

REID: Well, who wants to know?

BURRELL: Martin Burrell, the Minister of Agriculture. I was in
                my riding in the Okanagan so the Prime Minister
                asked me to look in on you.

REID: How do you do? Please convey my best wishes to the Prime Minister and, might I just say—

BURRELL: What the hell is going on here?

REID: They're hoping they'll get to see the *Rainbow* in action, Mr. Burrell.

BIRD: *(Off.)* Reid!

BURRELL: Who's that?

REID: *(With contempt.)* Bird. The passengers' lawyer.

BIRD: *(Coming on.)* I have Gurdit Singh's demands along with a list of provisions required before the boat will set sail.

> *Sheet of paper handed over.*

REID: It's as bad as before, dammit! That old coot actually thinks he's in a position to demand?

BIRD: They have a good supply of coal left, if you plan to attack again.

REID: Let the navy fire one across her bow. That will bring a quick end to these damn negotiations.

BURRELL: Agreed.

> *Sheet of paper handed back.*

REID: What!

BURRELL: He can have the full list of provisions if he agrees to allow them to be delivered at a point beyond Canada's five mile limit.

BIRD: That's over two hundred miles from Vancouver by sea.

BURRELL: In exchange, I will ask the Prime Minister to consider paying the outstanding charter monies.

REID: This is madness!

BIRD: *(Moving off.)* I will convey your offer to my client and let you know.

REID: I intend to protest this to…to the King!

Press Room

Newspaper printing press.

NARRATOR: *Vancouver Daily Province*, July 21, 1914. Extra! Headline: Hindus Finally Reply They Are Ready to Surrender Rather Than Chance a Fight. The Hon. Martin Burrell, minister of agriculture, in the Borden government, was largely the director of negotiations this afternoon with the Hindus…

Ext. Sea Lion.

The tug's engines at full.

REID: *(Under his breath.)* You even agreed to pay the charter money!

BURRELL: The Prime Minister will consider it and I think I know what his answer will be. In the meantime, that boat will no longer be here.

HOPKINSON: You will be true to your word, sir? About the provisions?

BURRELL: The government of this country is always true to its word, Inspector Hopkinson.

A blast from the Komagata Maru's horn.

BURRELL: Look! The passengers. They're lined up on the bulwarks. And what's that in their hands?

REID: It looks like…shoes. They're shaking their blasted shoes at us. Bewildering race.

Int. Jail.

Jail cell door opens.

Footsteps enter.

HOPKINSON: *(Coming on.)* The guards say you were yelling in the night, Mewa. How much longer do you want to spend in this cell?

MEWA: It is not my freedom that I want, Mr. Hopkinson.

HOPKINSON: *(Music under...bridge to next scene.)* It's too late. The boat has gone with all of the passengers safely on board. So it is just your freedom at stake now.

MEWA: *(Thinks, then.)* Balwant Singh and two others, Harnam Singh and Bhag Singh.

HOPKINSON: I always knew who they were. See?

Paper shuffle.

HOPKINSON: I already filled in their names on your statement. But I needed it in writing. Sign there.

A fountain pen uncapped. Writing.

You're free to go.

Cell door being opened.

Int. Classroom

FIONA: ...Margaret O'Flaherty—

A squeal of delight followed by quick steps.

FIONA: Congratulations. Here is your certificate.

Applause.

FIONA: Lucy Chan—

The door bursts open.

FIONA: Mewa!

MEWA: *(Slightly drunk.)* I am sorry I am late, Miss Fiona.

FIONA: That's fine. Just take your seat.

Footsteps.

Congratulations, Lucy. Here's your certificate.

Applause.

Well, I certainly hope this has been a beneficial experience for you—

MEWA: Don't I get a certificate?

FIONA: Mewa, certificates are for those who successfully complete the course.

MEWA: IT IS NOT MY FAULT!

FIONA: Mewa! I would appreciate it if you would keep your voice down.

MEWA: Why are you denying me my paper?!

FIONA: Have you been drinking?

MEWA: I WAS FIGHTING FOR MY BROTHERS' FREEDOM!

FIONA: I appreciate that, but you did not attend all the classes, nor did you complete the assignments.

MEWA: You are just like the men who denied the boat entry!

FIONA: I can't just give you a certificate because you deserve it. You have to fulfill the requirements. And these women have. This was a special day for them, and me, and now you've gone and ruined it.

Music sting.

So you can just leave, if you please!

MEWA loudly gets up and slowly walks out of the room.

Int. Church basement.

HOPKINSON's
SON: I promise to do my best, to do my duty, to God and
                    the King, and to obey the Scout Law; To help other
                    people at all times; To keep myself physically
                    strong, mentally awake, and morally straight.

REID: I trust you, on your honour, to keep this promise.
                    You are now one of the great World Brotherhood of
                    Scouts. To your patrol, quick march!

                    New scouts returning to their waiting patrols.

                    Applause.

                    *Dissolve to: Gentle murmur from parents drinking
                    tea.*

REID: *(Coming on.)* Ah—Hopkinson. What do you think of
                    young Simon?

HOPKINSON: I'm very proud of him.

REID: He's much fairer than you.

HOPKINSON: He takes after his mother.

REID: Have you ever been back home, lad? To see your
                    papa's birthplace?

HOPKINSON's
SON: I've never been to England. But I shall finish my
                    schooling there, right?

REID: England? No, no. That's not the place. Is it
                    Hopkinson? It's becoming quite a mystery, actually.
                    The India Office claims baptismal records there say
                    you were born in Delhi. To William and uh,
                    "Agnes" Hopkinson, then residing in Allahabad.

HOPKINSON: All this investigation so my son can join the Boy
                    Scouts?

REID: *(Snorting.)* It was your attitude towards the business
                    with the Hindoos. Perhaps that's why you have so
                    much difficulty with your loyalties.

HOPKINSON: *(Seething, under his breath.)* This is outrageous.

REID: You could settle the question once and for all by making it clear those people on the boat are as dangerous as I feared.

HOPKINSON: The boat is long gone!

REID: You would finally serve the department, for once— *(Moving off.)* and yourself in the bargain.

Dissolve to: Ext. Docks, Budge Budge—Night

> *Ship's horn as it arrives in port.*

DONALD: Attention passengers of the *Komagata Maru*. As District Magistrate of Calcutta, it is my duty to inform you that the Ingress to India Ordinance gives the Viceroy the power to arrest anyone entering the country if it is judged necessary to protect the safety, interest or tranquility of the state...

> *Dissolve to: Crowd muttering.*

EASTWOOD: *(English accent.)* Mr. Donald sir, thirty of my men can't hold them all. You better call for reinforcements before all hell breaks loose.

> *Dissolve to: Among the crowd. Passengers, weary, tense and angry.*

GURDIT
SINGH: All day and all night they have kept us sitting here. After all we have gone through...

MUNSHI: I just want to see my wife again. I wonder if she received my letter.

GURDIT
SINGH: Munshi, as soon as you get home, you must get to work—starting a family. Never forget, we outnumber them!

Distant marching.

MUNSHI: What's that?

Dissolve to:

EASTWOOD: One hundred and fifty Royal Fusiliers! Well, at least that's enough men to keep order now.

DONALD: Right. Then I'll talk to him. *(Calling.)* Gurdit Singh! Gurdit Singh!

GURDIT
SINGH: *(Off.)* What do you want?

DONALD: Come here, please.

GURDIT
SINGH: *(Off.)* I can speak to you where I am!

DONALD: In private, if you please.

GURDIT
SINGH: *(Off.)* I hide nothing from my brothers.

EASTWOOD: Leave it to me, sir. *(To GURDIT SINGH.)* Well, if you won't come when you are called, *(Moving off right.)* I'll just have to come and get you then!

> *Crowd murmuring as EASTWOOD wades into them.*

> *Begin slow fade under narrator and hold as background.*

One side, one side!

Crowd shouting.

(Off.) Whoa!

DONALD: Eastwood! Eastwood! I can't see you. Sit down, some of you!

More shouts.

A single shot rings out, from left close on to indicate police firing.

Passengers felled by shots. Cries, bodies hitting the ground.

Dissolve to: Press Room

Newspaper printing press.

NARRATOR: *(V.O. above.) Vancouver Daily Province*, October 1, 1914. Headline: Sixteen *Komagata Maru* Desperadoes Are Killed. The Sikh passengers on the steamer *Komagata Maru*, arrived at Bajbaj last Saturday. Some of them refused to board a train for the Punjab and opened fire with their revolvers. Troops were compelled to fire to check the rushes of the Sikhs...

Dissolve to: Governor of Bengal.

GOVERNOR
OF BENGAL: *(English accent.)* The Government of Bengal deeply deplores the loss of life which has occurred. Needless to say, no one had the smallest suspicion that any of the party were armed for a desperate attack on British officers...

Dissolve to: Music to underscore letter...

MUNSHI's
WIFE: Gulpur, September 30. My dearest Mewa. I never dreamed that my first letter to my brother-in-law would bear this news. Munshi is dead. He was shot in a riot on the docks when his boat landed. That is all they will tell me. They say over seventy others were shot, many killed. I will attend a gathering at Jullianwallah Bagh to protest. People are calling Munshi a hero. I wish he had never heard of Canada...

Int. Gurdwara—day.

Prayers and weeping, (all male).

Granthi and musicians singing funeral dirge.

Int. Gurdwara cloakroom—continuous.

Prayers and music in background

Scuffle.

Kirpan being drawn.

BALWANT
SINGH: Your time has come, Mewa Singh. They would all be alive if you hadn't betrayed us.

MEWA: Balwant Singh... If I believed that, I would use your kirpan to kill myself. Your guns would not have been enough against the British.

MEWA slammed against the wall.

BALWANT
SINGH: Then prove your loyalty.

MEWA: How?

BALWANT
SINGH: Kill Hopkinson's man, Bela. But make it soon. I will not give you a second chance.

MEWA: *(A sudden gasp.)*

BALWANT
SINGH: That blood on your cheek. *(Moving off.)* Will remind you.

The funeral dirge reaches a climax.

Int. HOPKINSON's office—day.

A knock on the door.

HOPKINSON: Yes?

Door opens.

HOPKINSON: *(With a heavy heart.)* Mewa. Sit.

> *Door closes.*

> *A few steps and a chair is moved as MEWA sits.*

> What happened to your face?

MEWA: It does not matter.

HOPKINSON: Is everyone at the gurdwara?

MEWA: Mm.

HOPKINSON: Would it be acceptable if I went there later?

MEWA: Gurdwara is open to all.

HOPKINSON: Mewa—

MEWA: I need to know something, Mr. Hopkinson.

HOPKINSON: What?

MEWA: Why did my brother die?

HOPKINSON: According to the report, the passengers had guns. Somehow Balwant got them on the boat after all.

MEWA: That is not why he died. I think it was his fate.

HOPKINSON: I tried to help him.

MEWA: You are just one man. I am just one man. Our "friendship" is not enough against fate.

HOPKINSON: ...Or the British army.

MEWA: Balwant Singh suspects my loyalty.

HOPKINSON: I have the same problem with Mr. Reid.

MEWA: He wants me to kill Bela. In fact, he is insisting.

> *HOPKINSON extracts some banknotes from his wallet.*

HOPKINSON: Use this money to buy the gun from him.

MEWA: Why don't you just arrest him? I will testify he told me to kill Bela.

HOPKINSON: I want him charged with sedition. By getting guns to the boat, Balwant made those men terrorists like him.

MEWA: My brother was a farmer.

Chair scrapes on the floor.

Footsteps.

Door opens.

(Off.) This is the last thing I shall do for you, Mr. Hopkinson.

Door closes.

Int. BALWANT SINGH's room—day.

BALWANT
SINGH: A nickel-plated .32 caliber revolver and a snub-nosed revolver. They should do the job. I would just give them to you—

MEWA: Here is the money. *(Moving off.)* Use it for a good cause.

Footsteps.

Door opens. Closes.

Press Room

Newspaper printing press.

NARRATOR: *Vancouver Province*, October 3, 1914. The partially decomposed body of a Hindoo man was found near the railroad tracks on the Kitsilano Indian reserve a few miles west of downtown Vancouver today. His turban was tied around his feet and his throat had been slashed from ear to ear. He was identified as Balwant Singh, one of the leaders of the seditionist movement in Vancouver's Indian colony. Bela Singh, another of the seditionists has been charged with his murder.

Int. Jail cell—day.

Cell door opening.

BELA: *(Chuckling.)* What are you doing here?

MEWA: *(Coming on.)* Why did you do it, Bela Singh?

BELA: Do what?

MEWA: Why did you kill Balwant?

BELA: There is no proof I did anything. And I will not be convicted. Mr. Hopkinson will see to that.

MEWA: Yes, I think the world lets men like you live a long life.

BELA: I am the only man who ever said the truth to you. Yet you hate me.

MEWA: You took away my dreams.

BELA: No, I took away your illusions. Now you can see the world clearly. And that makes you a free man.

MEWA: How can I be free if we are not all free?

BELA: That is your fate. Be grateful.

MEWA: It is not enough to be grateful.

BELA: It is enough for the wise man.

MEWA: It is enough for the coward.

Footsteps leaving.

BELA: Where are you going?

MEWA: The criminal assizes began last week. All the witnesses for your trial must report to the courthouse each morning.

BELA: Oh, then you will see Mr. Hopkinson. Say hello to him for me.

Echoing footsteps recede down corridor.

Int. Provincial Courthouse, Vancouver.

Courthouse ambience: Footsteps on marble, muted, echoing voices.

MEWA: *(Coming on.)* Mr. Hopkinson.

HOPKINSON: Another wasted morning, Mewa. Bela Singh's case was not brought forward, yet again.

.32 caliber shot fired at point blank range.

(Gasps.)

Screams from onlookers.

MEWA clubs HOPKINSON over the head with the revolver. Then drops it on marble floor.

Snub nosed revolver firing until chamber is empty. Click-click-click.

More screams.

JANITOR: Argh! That'll be all, you sammy bastard!

Scuffling.

MEWA: I'm finished, I'm finished. Take me to the station.

Dissolve to: Ext. Hastings Street—Day

Military band playing funeral dirge.

Solemn marching.

NARRATOR: *Vancouver Daily Province,* October 26, 1914. The body of Inspector W.C. Hopkinson was cremated at Mountain View cemetery on Saturday afternoon, after having been followed through the streets by one of the largest funeral processions ever held in this city. More than two thousand persons took part in the march as a mark of respect to the man who had laid down his life for the maintenance of law and order.

> *Int. MEWA's cell—day.*
>
> *Jail door opens.*
>
> *Footsteps.*

JAIL GUARD: *(Coming on.)* He has to put these on, Padre.

> *Ankle chains and handcuffs being put on.*

PRIEST: There's still time, Mewa. I can offer you absolution if you will convert.

MEWA: Will absolution save me from my fate?

PRIEST: Man can't forgive you, but God will.

MEWA: My fate is my creation. I do not expect forgiveness. I am a Sikh and what I have done will earn my place in heaven with our gurus who also martyred themselves for justice.

PRIEST: You are condemning yourself to eternal damnation.

MEWA: If I am to go to hell for my action, I will not be alone there either.

> *MEWA, shackled, shuffles out with guards and the priest.*

PRIEST: In nomine Patris, et Filii, et Spiritus Sancti...

> *Cross fade to:*

NARRATOR: Mewa Singh was hanged on January 11, 1915. He

was the first Indian to be executed in Canada. His picture hangs on the wall of the Vancouver gurdwara to this day.

Door clangs shuts. Footsteps echoing.

Fade out.

The End.

Couscous

Guillaume Vigneault

translated by John Van Burek

Guillaume Vigneault

Guillaume Vigneault was born in Montreal in 1970, and is the son of legendary Québec folksinger Gilles Vigneault. He studied literature at l'Université du Québec à Montréal, and cites Camus, Hemingway and Dostoyevsky as influences on his fiction. He has published two highly regarded novels, *Carnets de naufrage (Diary of a Shipwreck)* and *Chercher le vent (Looking for the Updraft)*.

About the Play

Marie-Claude is a young mother, a professional. She shares custody of her daughter, Andrée-Anne with her ex, Philippe. She is going to meet Aziz, a North-African (Maghrében) immigrant and the school soccer instructor for Andrée-Anne.

The play opens with Marie-Claude and her friend and colleague Sophie, chatting over a drink in a very lively bar.

Cast

MARIE-CLAUDE: .... Louise Gauthier

SOPHIE: .... Gisele Rousseau

AZIZ: ....Billy Khoury

ANDRÉE-ANNE: .... Isabelle Herington

PHILIPPE: .... Julian Doucet

Production Credits

Producer/Director: .... James Roy

Associate Producer: .... Colleen Wooods

Casting: .... Linda Grearson

Recording Engineer: .... Joe Mahoney

Sound Effects: .... Matt Wilcott

Scene 1

> *Interior, bar, music, conversations, glasses on the bar top, cash registers, etc.*

SOPHIE: *(Raising a toast.)* Alors, no Andrée-Anne till Sunday… That will be good for you. It's been a long time, n'est-ce pas? Attention, single mother in heat, watch out!

MARIE-CLAUDE: *(Sighs with a laugh.)* Yeah, sure…coute, it was very sweet of you to take me out, Soph, but honestly, you might have chosen another bar. We look like two old aunts!

SOPHIE: Marie-Claude, don't be so paranoid. Vraiment. We look just as young as all these girls, and I guarantee you, we're far more interesting, and what's more…er, we can hold our drinks a lot better! What more do you want?

MARIE-CLAUDE: "We can hold our drinks?" Christ, Sophie, you think that's a plus for us?

SOPHIE: Ben non, I'm only saying… Ah, pis, that's your problem, ma vieille. Anyway, my guess is that you'll be proven wrong in, oooh, about ten seconds, max…

MARIE-CLAUDE: Meaning…?

SOPHIE: Meaning, shut up! Starboard bow. Y chromosome…

AZIZ: Bonsoir, mesdemoiselles. May I offer you a drink?

SOPHIE: *(Lighting up.)* Bonsoir! A drink… I don't know, peut-être…

MARIE-CLAUDE: Mesdemoiselles... Nobody says that anymore. Nowadays, we use "madame"...

SOPHIE: *(In a firm tone.)* Oui, c'est vrai, ça! Do you want to start over and try that again, just to see...?

AZIZ: *(Laughing.)* Ah bon, fair enough, mesdames, so... Can I still offer you a drink m... mesdames?

MARIE-CLAUDE: *(With a slight laugh.)* D'accord, if you insist.

AZIZ: *(To the waiter.)* Two more of the same for les... *(Tongue-in-cheek.)* demoiselles, s'il vous plaît... But it's kind of sad, don't you think, that we can't say "mademoiselle" anymore? In fact, I don't get it...

SOPHIE: Really, you don't get it?

MARIE-CLAUDE: Sophie...

SOPHIE: Non, non! Monsieur wants to know why; we've got to tell him! *(To AZIZ.)* Because, mon cher monsieur, implicit in that is the idea that there is a difference between a married woman and an unmarried woman, and that, because this distinction doesn't exist when talking to a man, the distinction is, *de facto*, sexiste.

AZIZ: *(Ironic, but amused.)* Ah, ben, now I understand...

SOPHIE: Bon! I'm glad we've got that cleared up! And other than that, what is it you do, monsieur?

AZIZ: Eh bien, let's say that since arriving here, I've been coaching "soccer" as you call it.

MARIE-CLAUDE: *(A slight mocking tone, but lighting up.)* Ah, "since arriving here..." Meaning that before, in your own country, vous étiez, non, let me guess...engineer, I bet...

SOPHIE: Calvaire! Marie-Claude, you're terrible...! *(Making an announcement.)* She's cut off, OK??

AZIZ: *(Laughing.)* Non, ça va, it doesn't bother me. Actually, that was pretty good. Mais non, I wasn't an engineer... In fact, I was a coach there, too... but for football.

MARIE-CLAUDE: Soccer, football, pour vous autres, aren't they the same thing?

AZIZ: Ouais, but I can adapt, vous voyez... *(Ironic.)* Madame...

MARIE-CLAUDE: Ah, that's neat, because my daughter plays soccer, at her school.

AZIZ: Oui, je le sais. Andrée-Anne, right? As a matter of fact, I'm her coach... Je m'appelle Aziz. I think we've already met, haven't we?

SOPHIE: *(Superstitious tone.)* Oh, oh, oh, les coincidences... Marie-Claude, you know what I think about that...

MARIE-CLAUDE: Oui, oui, Soph. I know. But if you ask me, Monsieur has kind of strong armed les coincidences... Enchantée. I'm Marie-Claude.

SOPHIE: *(With a shy little voice.)* Et moi, je m'appelle Sophie. But that's OK, me, I'm going to get up and dance... I'll leave you two to talk about...soccer.

MARIE-CLAUDE: *(After a pause.)* Vous savez, Andrée-Anne just *a-dores* you. She... *(Laughing.)* As a matter of fact, she has a bit of a crush on you. But you didn't hear that from me, hein, on se comprend, là?

AZIZ: *(Laughing, a bit embarrassed.)* Ah, if only I were eight years old...

MARIE-CLAUDE: *(Feigning shock.)* If you were eight years old, cher monsieur, you'd have to deal with her mother!

AZIZ: I'd be a bit young for her mother, tout de même...

MARIE-CLAUDE: *(Flirtatiously.)* Well, you're already a bit young for her mother. *(Marking a beat.)* But just a little...

AZIZ: Just a little, hein? *(The laugh together.)* Alors, santé, Marie-Claude.

                 They toast one another.

MARIE-CLAUDE: Alors, football players, can they dance, too?

AZIZ: I was about to suggest the same thing. I will have to get used to this...

MARIE-CLAUDE: To what?

AZIZ: *(Lagging.)* To being asked to dance...

                 Bridge: Music louder, perhaps accompanied by singing. Songs to be determined. Then, fade-out music.

MARIE-CLAUDE: *(Out of breath.)* Whew! I haven't been this warm in a long time... Tu sais, I'm going to be real boring, Aziz, but I think I've had my fill of noise for tonight...

AZIZ: *(Also out of breath.)* Ouais, I think I've had enough dancing, too... Can I... Can I accompany you?

MARIE-CLAUDE: *(Insinuatingly.)* Euh... ça dépend... How far...?

AZIZ: *(Laughing.)* Just outside...

MARIE-CLAUDE: *(Bothered.)* OK, but I really must say goodnight to my friend... *(She hesitates.)* I can't see her... Ah, pis non, I'll call her tomorrow...

                 They make their way through the crowd.

AZIZ: Tiens, before we go out the door, I've got a question for you...

MARIE-CLAUDE: What?

AZIZ: Umm...is it frowned upon here, to open the door for a lady?

MARIE-CLAUDE: Ben voyons! Of course not!

AZIZ: *(Laughing.)* I'm only asking, you know, because a while ago, I held the door for some girl and she looks at me and says: "I can open my door toute-seule, merci!" so, I thought I should check.

MARIE-CLAUDE: *(Bursts out laughing.)* Well, ça dépend...

AZIZ: On what?

MARIE-CLAUDE: I don't know, maybe the way... C'est subtil.

AZIZ: *(Innocently.)* Ah bon...I don't know twenty-five ways of opening a door... But like this, is this OK? C'est assez subtil?

A door opens. Sounds of the city, fade-out music.

MARIE-CLAUDE: *(Tongue-in-cheek.)* Très bien, merci! But for la subtilité...I'm not too sure...

They go down the stairs.

AZIZ: Can I drop you somewhere?

MARIE-CLAUDE: *(With a slight laugh.)* Non, c'est gentil, but I'll just grab a cab at the corner... I think...maybe we've opened enough doors for tonight...

AZIZ: *(Laughing a little, slightly embarrassed, finding his words.)* Eh bien, je... Alors, euh, oui...

MARIE-CLAUDE: *(Teasingly.)* You're cute when you don't know what to say...

AZIZ: OK, OK, ça va faire. Alors...

MARIE-CLAUDE: *(Laughing again.)* Non, vraiment, you really are funny... I've got your number. I'll call you. Ciao.

She gives him a kiss. Moves away.

AZIZ: *(In a soft voice.)* OK, ciao. *(He laughs.)*

Scene 2

Interior, day. MARIE-CLAUDE's apartment. The phone rings several times.

MARIE-CLAUDE groans in a sleepy voice. She gets up. Fumbles around. Answers phone.

MARIE-CLAUDE: *(Pasty voice.)* Mmmm. Allo?

SOPHIE: *(Playing shocked.)* Oh la la! It's eleven o'clock! What *did* you do last night? I was calling your cell all evening!

MARIE-CLAUDE: Dead battery.

SOPHIE: *(Sceptical.)* Ouais, ouais, bien sûr… Anyway, you missed out on a fabulous evening last night, chez Christian. But you might have called me, quand même…

MARIE-CLAUDE: Sorry, I was busy…

SOPHIE: *(Third degree.)* Busy, mmm?… C'est qui?

MARIE-CLAUDE: *(Sighing.)* Nobody.

SOPHIE: OK, but just promise me, it wasn't Philippe, hein?

MARIE-CLAUDE: *(Bursts out laughing.)* Are you crazy?

SOPHIE: Phew! Attends… *(She has an idea.)* Not the soccer prof from last week?!?

MARIE-CLAUDE: Later, Sophie, OK?… *(Imploring.)* Let me have my coffee first, *sivousplait*…

SOPHIE: *(Triumphantly.)* Le prof de soccer!

MARIE-CLAUDE: Look, I can't talk now, OK?

SOPHIE: So he slept at your place?

MARIE-CLAUDE: *(Laughs, exasperated.)* I'll talk to you later, OK? I'm hanging up, now. Bye.

SOPHIE: *(As an order.)* You make yourself a coffee, then you phone me right back.

MARIE-CLAUDE: Oui, oui, oui. Bye.

She hangs up and sighs.

AZIZ: *(From the other end of the room.)* You're up, are you?

MARIE-CLAUDE turns on a tap to fill a glass of water.

MARIE-CLAUDE: No, not really. Do you want some water? I'm coming back to bed.

AZIZ: Oui, je veux bien.

Scene 3

Interior, day. Cafeteria. SOPHIE and MARIE-CLAUDE at work, are having a coffee together.

SOPHIE: *(With a tone of interrogation.)* Ouais, ouais, things seem to be going just fine with our prof de soccer... How long has it been now? *(Taking a pause.)* Ah, je le sais because for two whole months I've been trying to make a date with you to go to that new sushi place that I found... Deux mois! But that's OK, j'ai compris, we'll just have to go all three of us together...

MARIE-CLAUDE: No, no, I'll find us an evening. I've been really busy. But Thursday should be OK. Ça te va, jeudi?

SOPHIE: Ouais, but I'm holding you to it! Thursday it is, and there, I've put it in my book, c'est sérieux, là. "Thurs-day, din-ner Mar-ie-Claude." Voilà.

MARIE-CLAUDE: C'est un date.

SOPHIE: *(Teasingly.)* Oui madame. But... it's a bit suspicious: that was too easy, old girl... Thursday, mmm, wait a minute, that wouldn't happen to be the day that Muslims aren't allowed to screw, is it?

MARIE-CLAUDE: Don't be stupid.

SOPHIE: *(Innocently.)* What do you mean?

MARIE-CLAUDE: Aille, I know what you're up to, Sophie Perreau! You're fishing, you want tous les détails... And there's nothing subtle about you...

SOPHIE: *(Innocently.)* I have no idea what you're talking about. Des détails, franchement! What do you take me for, a teenager? I know what it's all about, so you and your sex life, I couldn't care less... *(In a conspiratorial voice, after a beat.)* No, but sérieusement...how is he?

MARIE-CLAUDE: *(Laughing.)* I knew it... You know I hate talking about this kind of thing...

SOPHIE: *(Disinterested.)* I'm not asking for positions! Just if... je sais pas...if it's good, generally speaking...

MARIE-CLAUDE: *(With hesitation.)* Well sure, it's.... it's good, yes.

SOPHIE: Ouhhh, là!

MARIE-CLAUDE: *(Irritated.)* What do you mean "Ouh, là?"

SOPHIE: Sorry, girl, but if you could see the look on your face, hein? 'Cause là, là, you're giving lots of details...

MARIE-CLAUDE: It's *good*, and that's it, OK? Now can we change the subject?

SOPHIE: OK, OK... It's just "good." Note taken. Fini. On n'en parle plus. New subject. *(Pause.)* And I suppose he has met Andrée-Anne?

MARIE-CLAUDE: *(Sighing.)* He already knows Andrée-Anne, you know that.

SOPHIE: Bon, bon, let me rephrase that, because we don't seem to be on the same wavelength...or you're not being straight with me: *(Spelling it out.)* Does Andrée-Anne know that her prof de soccer is her mother's new beau?

MARIE-CLAUDE: *(Sighs, without answering.)*

SOPHIE: OK, je comprends...videmment, your parents haven't met him, nor has Philippe, I take it...

MARIE-CLAUDE: *(Angrily.)* Ben là! Why would you want Philippe to meet him? It's none of his bloody business!

SOPHIE: Take it easy! He introduced you to his girlfriend, non? You are adults, pas vrai?

MARIE-CLAUDE: Ben, let's say we have different notions of what's right and wrong, hein? I mean, what can I tell you?... Besides, if you want to talk about "les adultes" I don't think his girlfriend fits in...

SOPHIE: Hé, hé! Fais pas ta bitch, là, you know it's not good for you. I mean, it's you who told me, just six months ago, "Sophie, don't let me get bitchy with her." Anyway, she's twenty-five years old and she's a charming girl. So, suck it up and move on. Don't be old Aunt Mildred.

MARIE-CLAUDE: *(A child's voice.)* Oui, d'accord Sophie, merci Sophie...

SOPHIE: Booon! So, when is it that you will allow Aziz *(An emphatic tone, tongue in cheek.)* to enter into your life...?

MARIE-CLAUDE: "To enter into my life!" Good God! Sophie! Write psychobabble books or, I don't know, soap operas or something, you are so clichéd...

SOPHIE: Yeah, yeah, "enter into your life." Have breakfast with. Introduce him to your daughter. Leave your tampons at his place. You know, the big romantic affair?

MARIE-CLAUDE: Non, c'est pas comme ça. I'm fine the way I am, just fine...our lives are nicely separated, tu comprends? It's simple, and for the moment, I don't want anything else...

SOPHIE: *(Doesn't answer.)*

MARIE-CLAUDE: And what is that look?…

SOPHIE: What look? The one that means: "I don't believe you for a second?" Is that the look you're talking about?

MARIE-CLAUDE: Pff! You don't *want* to believe me, that's your problem…

SOPHIE: Ben justement, I'd love to believe you. But your little refrain about "he's just a lover, I don't want any more, etc.," that's getting a bit tired. You're going to have to start asking yourself why, and *honestly*, why you don't want him in your life.

MARIE-CLAUDE: *(Tired.)* Oh, not you too…

SOPHIE: What do you mean, "me, too?" Aaah, he's getting impatient, is that it?

MARIE-CLAUDE: *(Reluctantly.)* Mouais… He thinks that… Ah, it's so stupid… *(Sarcastically.)* Monsieur thinks that it's cultural.

SOPHIE: *(Cautiously.)* Well…in his shoes, I might think the same.

MARIE-CLAUDE: *(Astonished.)* Are you serious?!?

SOPHIE: What do you expect him to think? That it's 'cause he teaches phys-ed in a grade school, or because… I don't know, he isn't part of what, your *world*, and all that? Franchement, you're the first one to say they're so boring, all these guys who come from the same milieu as you, the same jobs, you know what I mean! Don't try to tell me you thought it was great that you and Philippe knew all the same people, that you'd been to the same schools, that even your former boyfriend had been his roommate… Aille… Non, vraiment, a soccer prof is perfect for you. So… what's left then? It's the famous "choc culturel," sweetheart! Mind you, I understand fully. Because all that Arab machismo is hardly my bag... *(Pause.)* Why are you smiling all of a sudden?

MARIE-CLAUDE: Non, rien... But, he's not so bad...

SOPHIE: Ouais, ben "not so bad" would already be too much for me...

MARIE-CLAUDE: *(Amused.)* Ben non, Sophie, everything is in... the way you deal with it. For instance, you can't say "pick up your damned plate, I'm not your mother!" You have to say "Honey, can you help me with this..."

SOPHIE: Ben là, you're just stroking his ego, that's like with any guy...

MARIE-CLAUDE: Mouais... I guess that is pretty ordinary, isn't it?... *(They laugh.)* But I get used to it. And it's even interesting, there's something strategic about it...

SOPHIE: *(Dubious.)* Ouais, nevertheless, you're bending over backwards for your boyfriend... You know, you have every right to find it difficult, the cultural gap...

MARIE-CLAUDE: In the first place, he's not my boyfriend. And secondly, there isn't really a gap. That's all just superficial...

SOPHIE: *(Interrupting.)* Ha! Marie, you're so politically correct, I want to scream, even worse, I'm gonna throw up! All this will blow up in your face, believe me... You know, pretending that all this stuff, these little things that just kind of bug you a bit, that they're only superficial, that...it's only a matter of adjustment, ben c'est de l'hypocrisie and you know it. Can't we ever come out and say things as we see them? For instance, to say outright that there's one hell of a gulf in comprehension between a Muslim man and a western woman? Can't we just admit that?

MARIE-CLAUDE: Ben voyons, Sophie, calm down...

SOPHIE: No, really, it makes me crazy, tout ça... All these , I don't know, precautions that we're always taking when we talk about cultural differences. We always have to be *so* careful, c'est fatigant. So we end up treating every difference the same way, as if they were just some minor distinctions, purely décoratives, and we act as if underneath all that there were no differences in our fundamental values, that whatever they are is merely cosmetic. But merde, it's like trying to drown a fish. I mean, look, I'm sure the Koran is a beautiful book, fabulous poetry, the whole bit, but it's still what it is, non?... Sure, I know, we've committed the worst horrors with Bible in hand, but we've kind of gotten past that. So all this cultural crossover stuff, I'm fine with it as long as we're talking cuisine, or, I don't know, architecture or something. But once we start talking stoning to death, or female circumcision, I'm sorry but moi, je débarque, and my little western values, spoiled rotten, atheistic, neurotic, compulsive consumer, and so on and so forth, well je m'excuse but those values, when all is said and done, are simply better, and basta, point final.

MARIE-CLAUDE: *(After a silence.)* Wow...

(She bursts out laughing.) Well, you know, Sophie, I wasn't planning to get stoned to death, if that's what worries you! Mon Dieu, aren't you heavy all of a sudden...

SOPHIE: *(Irritated.)* Ben non, but you know what I mean...

MARIE-CLAUDE: ...videmment, but you can tell yourself that if Aziz was some fondamentaliste, I wouldn't be with him, hein?... Besides, what would he be doing teaching soccer in a primary school in Rosemont, can you answer me that?

SOPHIE: *(Jokingly conspiratorial.)* Maybe on an undercover mission…for al-Quaeda. In fact, you're his cover… Do you realise? Your boyfriend, a member of a sleeper cell…

MARIE-CLAUDE: My *lover*! T'es fatigante…

SOPHIE: *(Laughing.)* Aie, now that's something: for you, it's more a problem him being your boyfriend than being a terroriste…

MARIE-CLAUDE: *(Also laughing.)* Come on, don't I have the right to just have a frigging lover? Maudit, you're a real pain in the butt…

SOPHIE: Ben oui, nobody says you can't have a lover. But a lover isn't someone you sleep with every time your daughter is with her father…and who stays over for coffee, en plus! I mean, morning coffee, that really is the test, hein…? And, a lover isn't someone who makes it impossible for your best friend to invite you out to a restaurant. Sorry, but that's a boyfriend. Look in the dictionary, ma fille.

MARIE-CLAUDE: Sure, we know… For you, a "lover" is that guy you saw three times and never even got his last name…

          They both laugh.

SOPHIE: *(Through her laughter.)* OK. Don't start on that again… I just have a bad memory… But I do know his name was Raphael…

MARIE-CLAUDE: Ouais… So, Raphael, what happened to him?

SOPHIE: Well, I lost his phone number, you see…

MARIE-CLAUDE: And…

SOPHIE: Ben, c'es vrai, I don't know his frigging name!

          They both burst out laughing again.

Scene 4

> *Int., day. MARIE-CLAUDE's bedroom. She and AZIZ are lying in.*

MARIE-CLAUDE: *(Whispering, affectionately.)* Are you still asleep?

AZIZ: *(Sleepy voice.)* Wait, let me think... No, I don't think I'm sleeping. Tu vois, I am wondering if it may have something to do with the fact I have a finger in my ear...

MARIE-CLAUDE: It's not my finger, it's a pen.

AZIZ: Ah bon? C'est normal, je presume... You always carry a pen, hein...?

MARIE-CLAUDE: *(Laughing.)* Ben no, I'm doing my crosswords, silly boy... Moi, my day has already begun...

AZIZ: Ouais, ben justement, have you ever thought of putting curtains in the windows?

MARIE-CLAUDE: *(Questioningly.)* Curtains?...

AZIZ: Yes, curtains, those things made of cloth that you hang up in front of windows...

MARIE-CLAUDE: *(Teasingly.)* Ah oui, so that one can sleep in like a lazy bones when one has drunk too much wine the night before?

AZIZ: Euh, oui, ça par exemple, or for les siestes... Siestas are good things, non? So yes, they are called *curtains*...

MARIE-CLAUDE: Siestas, siestas...do I look like someone from the tropics? Besides, we'd miss all that great morning sunlight! You know, the sun is very good for the morale. Chez moi, it's full sun, take it or leave it... Also, did you know that in Scandinavia, they've done studies on exposure to natural light and they've found...

AZIZ: *(Jokingly.)* Oh! And I suppose I look like a Scandinavian?

MARIE-CLAUDE: *(Laughing.)* Noooo... *(In a mocking tone of remonstrance.)* You look...like a Muslim who has drunk too much alcohol, and who deserves what he gets! That's not allowed...

AZIZ: Ah, OK, now would you lay off on that one for a while, please? It hurts enough as it is... And aren't you a good Catholic girl?

MARIE-CLAUDE: *(Jokingly.)* Ab-so-lu-ment.

AZIZ: Except for the pill... I hope?

MARIE-CLAUDE: *(With a little voice of repentance.)* Euh, yes, except for that...

AZIZ: And relations outside of marriage...

MARIE-CLAUDE: Ah, tiens, that too. Bon, now are you going to preach to me? I shouldn't think so...

> *We hear bodies moving beneath the sheets. She gives him a long kiss.*

AZIZ: *(Murmuring.)* Heretic...

MARIE-CLAUDE: Just wait, you ain't seen nothing yet...

> *They continue to kiss, and we guess at more. Then, the phone rings. MARIE-CLAUDE falls back onto the bed, grumbling.*

MARIE-CLAUDE: I'm not answering...

AZIZ: Ben non, answer it... I know you, if you don't, you're going to fuss about it...

> *She finally gets up and reluctantly answers the phone. She trips on something and curses. They both laugh. She answers. A silence.*

MARIE-CLAUDE: *(Angrily.)* What do you mean "now"? Là, tout de suite? You were supposed to bring her here at five o'clock! It's only two-fifteen, Philippe! Me, too, I have a life, calvaire!

PHILIPPE: *(Undistinguishable.)*

MARIE-CLAUDE: What do you mean "what do I mean by that"? I mean I have a life, c'est trop compliqué, ça? And it's no longer any of your business, my life, I hope you know that much...

Ben oui, she's my daughter. But that doesn't give you the right to ask me that kind of question. I don't meddle in your affairs. I trust you. For whatever that's worth...

(Worn down.) Ah, you wear me out, Philippe. OK, OK, bring her home. Yes, I will be here. You go to your maudit meeting, but don't you dare do this to me again. And you owe me... Oui, OK, bye. I said, bye!

She hangs up angrily, banging the phone several times.

(Apologetically, a bit embarrassed.) Aziz...

AZIZ: *(With sustained irritation.)* Ça va, Marie-Claude. I will... I'll just go for a coffee down at the corner. De toute façon, your coffee is pretty bad...

MARIE-CLAUDE: *(Trying to be funny, sounds of childish horseplay on the bed.)* So you don't like my coffee, hein?

AZIZ: C'est bon, now, stop it, please. I'm leaving, but don't ask me to find it fun, OK?

MARIE-CLAUDE: *(Troubled, she mumbles a bit. She speaks into her pillow, with a muffled voice.)* Ben non, forgive me, it's just... But I hope you understand, I just need a bit of time. It's not easy for Andrée-Anne, having a new guy around... I'm only trying to do things the right way.

AZIZ: *(Interrupting her.)* I told you, it's OK. Anyway, you're repeating yourself, I've heard all this already. *(He pauses.)* But you know, Andrée-Anne isn't that fragile. And between finding me here in the morning and having to live with your separation and the fights with her father, to be honest, I'm not sure which is more traumatising...

MARIE-CLAUDE: *(Threateningly.)* Aie, watch out, slippery ground. Don't you take too many liberties, hein?

AZIZ: *(After a moment, in spite of himself.)* Pardon. It's none of my business. Really, I'm sorry. But one of these days you will have to tell me just what it is you're so afraid of.

                 AZIZ gets up, gets dressed.

MARIE-CLAUDE: But of nothing, Aziz! That's not it!

AZIZ: *(Sighing.)* Alors, c'est quoi, Marie-Claude? And it's not just for Andrée-Anne that I say that, it's for everything else, too... Have you introduced me to your friends? Or to your family? Merde, this has been going on for three months! To me, it feels like it's starting to be something, pas toi?

MARIE-CLAUDE: *(Searching for her words, almost imploring.)* Aziz, écoute. I need time, that's all. I don't want to complicate things right away. Right now, it's very simple and that is just what I need. Just be patient a little.

AZIZ: Well, it's starting to be a lot, Marie-Claude. And it's starting to be quite a while that it's been very simple. Just a bit too simple... A bit too simple for me. *(Long silence. Then, voice lowered)* And what's more... *(He checks himself.)*

MARIE-CLAUDE: And what's more, what?... I want to know...

AZIZ: No, forget it.

MARIE-CLAUDE: That's too easy! "And what's more..." What?

AZIZ: Ben, tu veux que je te dise? *(Pause.)* I think that if my name were Stéphane Gagnon, or something like that, and that if I'd been born in...Lac St-Jean, I think you might have introduced me to your daughter by now...

MARIE-CLAUDE: *(Shocked.)* Wô, là! I am not like that, and if that's what you think, buster, then...then you haven't understood a thing!

AZIZ: *(Nailing her.)* I'm not so sure I haven't understood, I'm not sure at all. And what else do want me to think? You people are so much like that here. You are all so convinced that you don't possess a single gram of racism, that you are so welcoming, so tolerant, I mean merde, it's unbearable! Here, you eat a bit of couscous and all of a sudden you feel so connected, so open, vachement world beat, hein? But when it comes to me meeting your daughter, alors ça, c'est autre chose... What, are you afraid I'll make her wear a veil?

MARIE-CLAUDE: *(Upset.)* OK, OK, OK, you're completely paranoid; it's impossible to talk to you...

AZIZ: Not at all. Là, tu vois, we're talking right now, and it feels good that we are, at least to me... That's what talking is! It's not about always been in agreement, and congratulating each other for being in agreement... while we're eating our pig's feet stew...

MARIE-CLAUDE: *(A slight laugh.)* Pork hocks.

AZIZ: *(Dumbfounded.)* What?

MARIE-CLAUDE: Pork hocks. Not pig's feet. C'est ragout de pattes de co'hon *(With the French-Canadian accent.).*

AZIZ: *(Laughs, in spite of himself.)* Right. You're a pain in the ass, you know that?

They both laugh a little, holding back. The doorbell rings.

MARIE-CLAUDE: *(In a sudden panic.)* Merde! Meeeerde! Maudite merde! Aziz... *(Embarassed.)*Would you mind...

AZIZ: *(Incredulous.)* Wait a minute... You...you want me to go out the back way?!... Is that what you're asking me? Putain, I don't... *(He stops himself.)*

Doorbell rings again. Long silence.

MARIE-CLAUDE: *(Confused.)* Je...I'll call you tonight, OK? We'll talk about all this, listen, I understand, we'll talk about it, c'est...

AZIZ: *(Upset.)* Ça va, Ça va! *(He takes a beat.)* But there is one thing: going out the back way, I swear to you, it's the first and last time.

MARIE-CLAUDE: Je comprends. Honestly. *(A pause.)* Still, can I have a kiss?

AZIZ: *(Coldly.)* You just don't realise, do you?

AZIZ hurries out, sound of footsteps, then the back door slams. Again, the doorbell rings. MARIE-CLAUDE activates the buzzer.

MARIE-CLAUDE: *(Up-beat, forced.)* Salut ma chouette!

ANDRÉE-ANNE: Allo. I have to go to the bathroom, vite, vite, I can't talk to you.

Sounds of running in the hallway, door closing.

MARIE-CLAUDE: *(Laughs a bit, then, to PHILLIPE.)* Ouais, that was a very short fifteen minutes!

PHILIPPE: *(In a rush.)* Yeah, I know, excuse-moi. This landed on me this morning, I really have to run. A production meeting, it wasn't supposed to be...

MARIE-CLAUDE: *(Cutting him off.)* Never mind. I don't really care. Go ahead.

PHILIPPE: OK, ouais... *(With a loud voice, to his daughter.)* Bye ma puce!

ANDRÉE-ANNE: *(From far.)* Bye Papa!

PHILIPPE: *(To MARIE-CLAUDE.)* So...you'll take her on Friday?

MARIE-CLAUDE: *(Impatient.)* Vendredi, c'est ça. Bye.

PHILIPPE: OK.

                He scuttles down the stairs. MARIE-CLAUDE closes the door and sighs. At the same moment, the phone rings.

MARIE-CLAUDE: Allo?

ANDRÉE-ANNE: *(From the bathroom.)* M'maaan! There's no papier de toilette!

MARIE-CLAUDE: OK, j'arrive, just give me a minute! *(Back to the phone, irritated.)* Oui, pardon, hello?

AZIZ: Salut. Listen, I'm down on the corner, but I left my watch on the bedside table...

MARIE-CLAUDE: *(Embarrassed.)* Yes, but...uh, it's just that...

AZIZ: *(Cutting her off.)* Mais non, I'm not coming to get it! I'm telling you because Andrée-Anne always uses my watch to do the timings when we do our exercises... She's going to recognize it if she sees it. So put it away, that's all.

MARIE-CLAUDE: *(A bit thrown.)* Ah, oui... OK. Euh... merci.

AZIZ: Ouais, ça va. Allez, ciao... Pork-hocks... *(He hangs up.)*

Scene 5

> *Exterior, day. A soccer match. Cries of children, whistles blowing, crowds. PHILIPPE and MARIE-CLAUDE are watching ANDREE-ANNE's match. AZIZ is watching the game from the sidelines. We hear his voice, in the distance, calling advice to his players.*

PHILIPPE: So that's him, the great soccer coach…

MARIE-CLAUDE: *(Sounding a bit unsure.)* …Euh, oui, pourquoi?

PHILIPPE: *(Having a laugh.)* Oh, it's nothing… It's Andrée-Anne. She sure has a major crush on this guy.

MARIE-CLAUDE: *(Playing indifference.)* Oui, je le sais. It's always "Aziz this, Aziz that"…

PHILIPPE: Aziz, oui, that's his name. I couldn't remember. Have you met him?

MARIE-CLAUDE: Ben…sort of… *(Pause, then she laughs.)* You know what she asked me the other day? If Aziz and Papa ran a race, who would win?

PHILIPPE: And what did you tell her?

MARIE-CLAUDE: *(Laughing.)* Ben, là, Philippe… There is a limit…I told her that Aziz would probably win, *but* only just, and that he'd really have to run hard… That's about as far as I could stretch it, just between you and me…

PHILIPPE: *(Good naturedly.)* Ah, I'm not so sure… If I got back into shape…

MARIE-CLAUDE: Good, I'm glad to know you have so much free time…

PHILIPPE: It's just a matter of organization.

MARIE-CLAUDE: Ha! You, organized? Aille, you forget who you're talking to!

PHILIPPE:　　Bon, bon... Here we go again...

MARIE-CLAUDE:　Ben non, but don't just go talking through your hat...

> *A long moment. The parents watch the game. Shouts from the children, whistles blowing.*

PHILIPPE:　　*(Clearing his throat.)* Aille, look, euh... I'm going to have to leave... I didn't expect this to last so long...

MARIE-CLAUDE:　Now this is the second game where you pull this on me, you know that? Then who is it has to explain to Andrée-Anne why you couldn't stay?

PHILIPPE:　　*(In a bind.)* Listen, I promised Christine that...

MARIE-CLAUDE:　*(Bitter.)* Christine, hein? You promised Christine... And what about Andrée-Anne, you didn't promise her you'd come to watch her game? But hey, c'est correct, Andrée-Anne is seven years old, what the heck, she'll understand... Pauvre Christine is only twenty-six, alors, we have to be careful not to hurt her little feelings...

PHILIPPE:　　Calvaire, Marie-Claude... Is there no way for things to be simple, just once in a while?

MARIE-CLAUDE:　*(Incredulous.)* Ben oui, c'est ça... it's all my fault. At least say good-bye to your daughter. She's right over there, and look, there's a time out...

PHILIPPE:　　*(Calling over to ANDRÉE-ANNE.)* Andrée-Anne! Andrée-Anne! *(While he's waiting.)* Will you look at her, the little smartypants... She's going to introduce me to her coach... *(He laughs.)*

ANDRÉE-ANNE:　*(Arrives out of breath.)* Papa, did you see the pass I made to Myriam? Did you see that, when, euh, when that girl got next to me, and then I passed it to Myriam, and that other girl, even though she's in third year! But Myriam, she can't really run fast, but she almost made it anyway...

PHILIPPE: Ben oui, you bet I saw it!

ANDRÉE-ANNE: Papa, this is my coach!

PHILIPPE: Ah, c'est lui?

AZIZ: Bonjour…

PHILIPPE: Enchanté! It's Aziz, if I'm not mistaken? I've sure heard a lot about you!

AZIZ: *(Suddenly ill at ease.)* Ah bon?… Euh, enchanté, oui…

MARIE-CLAUDE: *(Laughing nervously.)* Ah, oui, Andrée-Anne is always talking about soccer! I think this is the beginning of a great career!

                 They all laugh.

AZIZ: *(Relieved.)* Ah, oui, no question about that! One heck of a career!

PHILIPPE: *(To ANDRÉE-ANNE.)* Andrée-Anne… Papa is going to have to leave. It's a drag, I know…

ANDRÉE-ANNE: *(Disappointed.)* Ben là! You haven't even seen me score a goal yet!

PHILIPPE: I know, but you can tell me all about it on Tuesday, OK? And I took some pictures today, so they'll be ready then…

ANDRÉE-ANNE: *(Pouting.)* OK… Bye.

AZIZ: *(Up-beat, gently.)* Allez, Andrée-Anne, you're out there. Go on, get a move on! *(To PHILIPPE.)* Bien, au revoir, alors… It's too bad, this is a close game, it will be getting good…

PHILIPPE: *(Sighs.)* Ah, duty calls… But, it was a pleasure meeting you. Au revoir.

                 AZIZ goes. A moment of silence.

                 (Pointedly.) So, the soccer coach… eh ben, eh ben…

MARIE-CLAUDE: What?

PHILIPPE: *(Non-committal.)* Though mind you, that must be a change… *(He leaves a pause.)* Voyons donc, Marie-Claude, I know you pretty well, quand même! You should have seen how you were babbling just now, it was ridiculous…

MARIE-CLAUDE: *(After a pause, firmly.)* In any case, oui: it's an enormous change.

PHILIPPE: *(After a pause, light tone.)* And how old is he, twenty-five, max?

MARIE-CLAUDE: No. Thirty. But *he* gets exercise.

PHILIPPE: *(Ironic.)* Ouch! *(He laughs.)* And other than that, does Andrée-Anne know?

MARIE-CLAUDE: *(Forced calm.)* Non, elle le sait pas. I try not to upset her, *me.* And I'm counting on you to do the same, tu comprends?

PHILIPPE: *(Contemptuously.)* Ah, écoute, I couldn't care less, hein?… Though still, to have your first love stolen by your own mother…

MARIE-CLAUDE: Ah, shut your face!

                A long silence.

PHILIPPE: A soccer coach…

MARIE-CLAUDE: *(Between her teeth.)* Quoi "a soccer coach…?" What are you trying to say? That I could do better than that? Of course that's it…but even from you, it would be too crude to say so… But that's damn well what you're thinking, hein? But whoa, it looks bad on us when we vote left and then say things like that…

                (She leaves a pause.) So, oui, he's a soccer coach! And the last time that "I did better than that", ben, toi pis moi, we know how that turned out!

PHILIPPE: Du calme... Alright, excuse-moi, it was...uh *(Mockingly.)* très politically *in*correct of me...

MARIE-CLAUDE: Très ignorant jerk, you mean.

PHILIPPE: Et pis, euh, how long has this been going on?

MARIE-CLAUDE: That's none of your business.

PHILIPPE: Is it serious?

MARIE-CLAUDE: That's...still none of your business.

PHILIPPE: *(Snidely.)* And are you...planning to convert?

MARIE-CLAUDE: Quoi?

PHILIPPE: Ben...to Islam, you know, the veil, stonings, all those nice things...

MARIE-CLAUDE: *(Incredulous.)* Philippe, you are hal-lu-ci-na-tory! So, in fact, that's what you're worried about, hein?

PHILIPPE: Moi, I'm not worried about a thing! In the first place, I'm not a woman... *(Snickers.)* You can tell me more when you come back from Morocco...

MARIE-CLAUDE: Algérie. And no, I won't be talking to you. In fact, I don't even know why I'm talking to you now! Especially since all I get is you saying outrageous stuff like that... *(Nastily.)* You are such a moron, I've got to tell you, it almost gives me satisfaction...Au fond, it settles a lot of things for me... Merci, really.

PHILIPPE: *(Ironic.)* Oui, oui, c'est ça... You play the great, offended soul, I recognize you all too well... But aille, don't try to tell me that you don't have your own prejudices... Toi? The champion of internet petitions, to stop some lapidation somewhere in Nigeria, or the Sudan, forever beating me about the ears with all that crap...

MARIE-CLAUDE: Ah, Philippe, stop it. Between the two of us, if anyone ought to re-examine his prejudices, who might that be?

PHILIPPE: Ouais, we'll see about that, hein?

MARIE-CLAUDE: Ben, you know what, no we won't! Look, just go back to your Christine, là, 'cause she must be getting lonely, toute-seule avec elle-même...

PHILIPPE: Pff! *(He hesitates.)* I'm telling you, we shall see.

MARIE-CLAUDE: *(Laughing.)* C'est ça, salut!

> *MARIE-CLAUDE sighs. A long moment. AZIZ arrives.*

AZIZ: Salut... *(Hesitates.)* Euh...tout va bien?

MARIE-CLAUDE: Oui, ça va. He exhausts me.

AZIZ: Ouais.

MARIE-CLAUDE: *(Long sigh.)* He's figured us out. He's good at that stuff. I don't know why, but he understands fast...

AZIZ: *(Gently.)* I'm really sorry.

MARIE-CLAUDE: *(Resigned, not hostile.)* Ben non, it's OK. It just happened, that's all. It's OK... Vraiment.

AZIZ: You're sure?

MARIE-CLAUDE: *(Warmly.)* Yes, I'm sure. Merci.

> *The cries of children grow louder. Then, there is a sudden clamouring in the crowd. MARIE-CLAUDE joins in, as does AZIZ.*

> *(Clapping.)* Bravo! Bravo!

AZIZ: *(Moving away, heading toward the game.)* Ah, ouais! Ah ouais! That is a goal!

> *MARIE-CLAUDE is still applauding a little. Then, she suddenly takes out her cell phone and dials a number.*

MARIE-CLAUDE: *(Into the telephone, sarcastically.)* Oui, bonjour Philippe. *(With the voice of a teenaged air-head.)*

Bonjour Christine! This message is for Philippe. By the way, you have a funny accent on your answering machine…that must be le français *international*. Anyway, I just wanted you to know, Philippe, that your daughter just now scored a goal. Salut. *(She hangs up, then to herself:)* My God, you're so mature, Marie, sacrament…

Scene 6

> *Interior, day. SOPHIE and MARIE-CLAUDE are chatting over a glass of wine, chez MARIE-CLAUDE.*

SOPHIE: Ah non, you have to give Philippe credit for that… He can be very perceptive that way… But it's partly your fault, too, you're such a lousy liar!

> *They laugh.*

MARIE-CLAUDE: Oui, mais, I never intended to lie to him, I just didn't want him to realise that something was going on…

SOPHIE: I'd say that comes under the category of "lying", ma fille…

MARIE-CLAUDE: *(Laughs.)* Ouais, peut-être…

SOPHIE: So when was it, again, that all this happened?

MARIE-CLAUDE: Euh, ben, six days ago, now…

SOPHIE: Pis, t'as pas de nouvelles?

MARIE-CLAUDE: De Philippe? Oui, unfortunately… He must have called me eight times this week…

SOPHIE: To say what?

MARIE-CLAUDE: Ah, nothing, justement… Any pretext, des niaiseries. Andrée-Anne, her homework, the slightest scratch she might have gotten, that kind of thing… And through it all, bien sûr, are all these insinuations, these sous-entendus, every three sentences… He's trying to find out stuff by ricochet, you know what I mean… Ah oui, et la meilleure, listen to this: he tries to make me feel guilty because Andrée-Anne has a crush on Aziz! *(She laughs.)* Oh, and the other night, she asked me how old he will be by the time she's eighteen… She didn't like the answer! *(Laughter.)* Ça fait que, she decided he was too old for her.

SOPHIE: *(Laughing.)* Ah, that bugged you a little, quand même, hein?

MARIE-CLAUDE: Franchement…

SOPHIE: *(Finger-wagging.)* Marie-Claude…

MARIE-CLAUDE: Bon, OK, oui. A bit.

SOPHIE: But this Philippe stuff, why let him get away with that?

MARIE-CLAUDE: Ben, I feel a bit trapped. Put yourself in my place…

SOPHIE: Ouais… Mais tu sais, hein, the simplest thing would just be to come clean with it. I mean, with Andrée-Anne, aussi.

MARIE-CLAUDE: Aie! Is there some way, par hasard, that I can do things my way, and *in my own time*? Hein? I mean I'm not having my arm twisted by Philippe, goddamn it. Y a toujours des limites…

SOPHIE: *(Challenging her.)* Ben là, Marie-Claude, I don't call that "in your own time." Besides, are you going to put up with Philippe's little guerilla warfare?

MARIE-CLAUDE: *(Sighs.)* Non… Mais sérieusement, why do you keep pushing me on all this? *(Jokingly.)* Listen, how much does he pay you, my boyfriend, to lobby for him like this?

SOPHIE: Your *boyfriend*? Ah, ha!

MARIE-CLAUDE: Slip of the tongue!

SOPHIE: *(Triumphantly.)* A *big* slip, en tous cas... *(Getting serious again.)* ...coute, I'm not pushing you, sweetheart. Mais, j'sais pas, I just don't understand what you are doing...or what it is you're waiting for. I'm all for taking however long it takes. Mais, je te jure, a mere lover, at some point, can no longer become anything else. *(Knowingly.)* And between you and me, you're not afraid this won't work; you're afraid that it will. Tiens.

MARIE-CLAUDE: *(Laughing it off.)* Bon, bon...Sophie Perreau, drunken psychologist... *(Affectionately.)* Tu m'éneeeerves!

SOPHIE: Ah, *in vino veritas*... Bon, OK, I'll leave you alone... But my glass is empty. Do I open the other bottle?

SOPHIE gets up, goes to the kitchen.

MARIE-CLAUDE: It's four-thirty in the afternoon, Sophie...

SOPHIE: Pis après? It's a nice little rosé de rien, it won't bite... Besides, do you have anything better to do?

MARIE-CLAUDE: *(With a sigh.)* Ben oui, like supper, peut-être. Andrée-Anne will be home from school any minute. Ah, justement, I think that's her now.

The sound of footsteps in the stairway. MARIE-CLAUDE gets up and goes to the door. SOPHIE opens the wine bottle.

SOPHIE: Bon ben, old aunt Sophie's going to look like a wino, again.

MARIE-CLAUDE: What else is new...?

SOPHIE: *(Talking like a drunkard.)* I'll behave! I won't give any wine to the child, promis! Or maybe just a little glass... It's good for her arteries...

MARIE-CLAUDE: That's only red wine. Besides, I think her arteries are still new enough, ça va aller...

ANDRÉE-ANNE: *(Arriving, noisily, out of breath.)* Allo! Allo Sophie!

MARIE-CLAUDE: Hé cocotte, the school bag doesn't go on the floor... Mais... what happened to your bag?

ANDRÉE-ANNE: *(Unconcerned.)* Ah... C'est Lucie who tore it, but she didn't do it on purpose. And the teacher said it would be easy to fix.

MARIE-CLAUDE: Easy to fix... I don't have anything to fix it with...

SOPHIE: The shoemaker, down at the corner. It'll cost you five bucks.

ANDRÉE-ANNE: Five bucks, M'man, franchement! That's nothing!

MARIE-CLAUDE: *(Astonished.)* Bon... OK, I guess it's cheap, if Andrée-Anne says so... Mais Lucie, how did she manage to do that?

ANDRÉE-ANNE: I told you, not *on purpose!*

MARIE-CLAUDE: OK, OK... And c'est qui, this friend of yours?

ANDRÉE-ANNE: Ben, tu le sais, she's the girl who sits next to me. *Luciiie,* franchement.

MARIE-CLAUDE: Ben, Lucie, Lucie, how do I know?

ANDRÉE-ANNE: *(Sighs.)* Ben oui, she's got that green bike, the one that's so ugly!

SOPHIE: *(Laughing.)* Ben, Marie-Claude, franchement! The green bike!

ANDRÉE-ANNE: And she's the one who loaned me that book, tu sais, the one on whales!

MARIE-CLAUDE: Ah, ben là, I don't remember...

ANDRÉE-ANNE: *(Exasperated.)* M'man, you know her, franchement! I went to her birthday party...

MARIE-CLAUDE: Aaah! OK. The little Haitian girl! Well you could have said... *(She checks herself.)*

ANDRÉE-ANNE: *(After a beat, as if it were obvious.)* Ben oui...

SOPHIE: *(Biting her tongue to keep from laughing, putting on a
                   very professorial tone.)* Tiens, now that was an
                   "intergenerational moment", très intéressant…
                   sociologically speaking, bien sûr…

MARIE-CLAUDE: Shut up, you!

ANDRÉE-ANNE: *(Triumphantly.)* On dit pas "shut up," it's im-polite!

                   All three laugh.

ANDRÉE-ANNE: What does that mean, "sociologically?"

MARIE-CLAUDE: Never mind, Sophie is just being stupid. Don't even
                   listen to her… You can help me make supper,
                   instead.

ANDRÉE-ANNE: Pfff! You don't even know, toi même!

MARIE-CLAUDE: *(Pretending to be severe.)* He, toi! I'll give you… Je
                   t'avertis, you'll be peeling potatoes… Allez, s'il te
                   plaît, go wash your hands, ma chouette…

                   Sound of footsteps as ANDRÉE-ANNE walks away.

SOPHIE: *(Imitating MARIE-CLAUDE.)* "Aaah! OK! The little
                   Haitian girl…"

MARIE-CLAUDE: C'est correct, Soph. You can lay off. I grew up in
                   Gaspé, calvaire! There weren't any blacks… You
                   want me to apologize for that…?

SOPHIE: Ben non, forget I mentioned it! I grew up in
                   Sherbrooke, fait que… To tell you the truth, I think
                   it's great that that's the last thing to come into your
                   daughter's head when talking about her friend.
                   C'est formidable…c'est *encourageant*…

MARIE-CLAUDE: *(Teasingly.)*You're drunk…

SOPHIE: No connection. Mais bon, you come from Gaspé,
                   but now it's what, ten, twelve years that you're in
                   Montréal, and do you know any more blacks, now?

MARIE-CLAUDE: Pis toi?

SOPHIE: No, me neither, and that's what I'm saying, it's not a competition! I'm doing a *sociological study*...

MARIE-CLAUDE: Oh, come on... So what is it you are saying?

SOPHIE: Bah, rien. Une observation.

MARIE-CLAUDE: *(Suspicious.)* I can tell you're going to talk to me about mon arabe, là.

SOPHIE: You mean, your *boyfriend*? It's coming, inquiète-toi pas. Just another little glass. You are *so* not out of the woods yet... Au fait, do you know if Aziz likes sushi?

MARIE-CLAUDE: *(Feigning exasperation.)* Je le sais pas if he likes sushi! You don't let up, do you? Hein?... Sshhh!

                Sound of ANDRÉE-ANNE's footsteps. MARIE-CLAUDE and SOPHIE hide their laughter.

ANDRÉE-ANNE: Moi, j'aime ça les sushis...

SOPHIE: Quoi, you're only seven and you like sushi?

ANDRÉE-ANNE: Oui, but I didn't when I was little...

SOPHIE: *(Laughing.)* Ouais, I'm telling you, it would be pretty tough to traumatize this kid of yours...

MARIE-CLAUDE: Don't worry... You're about to do it to me...

ANDRÉE-ANNE: Cest quoi ça, traumatize?

MARIE-CLAUDE: *(Laughing.)* It's what your Aunt Sophie is doing to your pauvre maman... This is traumatizing, and she's not finished yet!

ANDRÉE-ANNE: *(Sounding on her guard.)* I'll just look it up in the dictionary, so there!

MARIE-CLAUDE: Good idea. Fais donc ça, Andrée-Anne.

Scene 7

> *Exterior, street, evening. MAIRE-CLAUDE and
> AZIZ coming back from an evening out, heading
> towards MARIE-CLAUDE's house. Footsteps on
> the sidewalk, traffic noises.*

MARIE-CLAUDE: Ah, moi, I don't want to see any more raw fish for a month. I really ate too much, but sushi always does that to me, I can't stop. *(She laughs.)* It's like with blueberries...

AZIZ: Ah bon, blueberries? But that really was good sushi, even though it was kind of expensive.

MARIE-CLAUDE: Kind of!! C'était ridicule! But that's Sophie, hein, every single restaurant chic that opens up on Saint-Laurent, she's got to try it... She's hoping she'll bump into George Clooney some day...

AZIZ: *(Laughing.)* Oh, t'est méchante!

MARIE-CLAUDE: Naw, I'm not... That's Sophie, it's just the way she is. But she makes no bones about it. Fait que... what did you think? You didn't find her too stiff... I mean with you?

AZIZ: Stiff? No, pas du tout. I thought she was lots of fun.

> *They walk along for a moment without talking.*

MARIE-CLAUDE: Sure, you the scrapper, ça te fait plaisir, ça...

AZIZ: *(Ironic, exaggerating the Maghreb accent.)* Ouais, ouais, we are all rug dealers, and all we do is squabble with one another... C'est notre sport national, if you like... "What's the matter with you? You want a punch in the nose?"

MARIE-CLAUDE: Don't be a jerk, that's not what I said... You're so paranoid, you...

AZIZ: *(Laughing.)* Ben non, I know...

MARIE-CLAUDE: But other than that, did you have fun tonight?

AZIZ: Ben oui, sure I did... Why wouldn't I?

MARIE-CLAUDE: Ben, je sais pas, but with Sophie, we always end up talking about work... I'm sure it's not much fun for you.

AZIZ: Ben...! Au contraire, I learn all kinds of things. Especially about you...

MARIE-CLAUDE: Ah oui? T'apprends des trucs, hein?... Like what?

AZIZ: Euh, you see, par exemple, I've learned that I really wouldn't want to be your boss, mmm? You sure don't make life easy for him...

MARIE-CLAUDE: Ah bon? Well that's fine, 'cause there's not much danger of that, is there? My boss, pff!

AZIZ: Mind you, I wouldn't mind, just the for the title... Then you could just call me "patron"... Allez, I'm sure you'd grow to like it...

MARIE-CLAUDE: Ohh, attention, toi. You're going to sleep on the sofa tonight...

AZIZ: I like your sofa... You know, that's something that girls never understand: tu vois, guys like to sleep on the sofa, it feels like we're out camping...

MARIE-CLAUDE: *(Bursts out laughing.)* Bon, then you can go sleep on the balcony, that'll feel encore plus réaliste!

               They both laugh. They stop in front of the door to MARIE-CLAUDE's apartment.

MARIE-CLAUDE: Bon, les clef, les clefs... *(She fishes in her bag.)*

AZIZ: *(Insinuating.)* Ah, I can't help you there...

MARIE-CLAUDE: I *know* you don't have one... *(Rattle of keys.)* Tiens, justement, you won't need one.

               She unlocks the door, sound of foot steps in the stairway.

AZIZ: *(Séducteur.)* I like it when you wear skirts like that…

MARIE-CLAUDE: *(Pretending to be shocked.)* Ben oui, hein, especially when seen from below on the stairs. Phallocrate…

> *She opens the upstairs door and enters the apartment. Sound of footsteps, keys on the table, etc.*

AZIZ: *(From a distance, he has gone into the bedroom.)* Non!… C'est pas vrai, I'm dreaming…

MARIE-CLAUDE: Quoi?

AZIZ: Curtains! You've bought curtains! I am truly touched…

MARIE-CLAUDE: They were on sale.

AZIZ: *(Voice back in proximity; with a child's voice.)* Des rideaux, pour moi…oh…

> *He gives her a kiss.*

MARIE-CLAUDE: Attends… You'll see, they're very, *very* transparent.

Scene 8

> *Interior, day. MARIE-CLAUDE's room. She and AZIZ are in the kitchen. MARIE-CLAUDE pours two cups of coffee. Sound of footsteps. Setting down of spoons.*

MARIE-CLAUDE: *(After a moment)* So, is it better, mon café?

AZIZ: Ah, ouais, I'll give you that… This is nothing like the… *(He laughs.)* that petroleum you usually make…

MARIE-CLAUDE: Petroleum, hein? You've got a nerve! En tout cas, this one is Fair Trade and believe me, it costs a fortune per kilo…

AZIZ: Ah, ha, c'est ça, the little after-taste: it's the flavour of Free Trade, of social justice… Ah, c'est pas mauvais…

MARIE-CLAUDE: Go right ahead, moque-toi... But in the meantime, there is some Columbian peasant who is growing coffee instead of working for the drug cartel...

AZIZ: Oh, la, la, tout ça, c'est trop compliqué pour moi! But your coffee is very good. In fact, I think I'll come back...

MARIE-CLAUDE: Ah, but you are not going anywhere in the first place, je te signale...

           The phone rings. MARIE-CLAUDE answers.

MARIE-CLAUDE: Allo?

PHILIPPE: *(Undistinguishable.)*...

MARIE-CLAUDE: *(Upset.)* Philippe, calvaire! This is Sunday! How do you manage to be so badly organized? *(She lets out a long growl.)*....

MARIE-CLAUDE: Pis Christine, elle, what does she do le dimanche? Her nails?....

MARIE-CLAUDE: *(Suddenly resigned and non-chalant.)* OK, c'est correct, bring her home...

MARIE-CLAUDE: *(Incredulous.)* Ah, and what's more, I have to take her there? ...Because *you* had promised to take her?!? *(She laughs.)* Aille, c'est fort, ton affaire, Philippe. You've really outdone yourself, this time. You are...attends...you are a real *goofball*, that's the word I was looking for. OK, see you in a bit. C'est ça. Bye.

           She hangs up. There is a long silence. The sound of a chair scraping on the floor.

AZIZ: Bon, I see it's starting all over again... *(He takes a deep breath.)* This really isn't working, is it?

MARIE-CLAUDE: *(Firmly.)* No, attends, stay.

AZIZ: *(Brusquely.)* For what? Five minutes? And to do what?

MARIE-CLAUDE: *(After a long silence.)* Because... Ah, pis merde! Because you have a car, and because imagine-toi, today I have to take my daughter to the Biodome. *(Silence. She gets up and approaches him. Then, with a gentle voice, almost whispered.)* Have you ever been to the Biodome?

AZIZ: *(With a small laugh.)* No.

MARIE-CLAUDE: You'll love it.

The End.

Appendix

Proposal Call for Radio Plays on the Topic of Immigration

CBC's radio drama program Sunday Showcase is soliciting proposals for a new series to be broadcast in the spring of 2005. This is a cross-cultural project in partnership with La Châine Culturelle, the cultural network of Radio-Canada. Sunday Showcase is Canada's national theatre and is heard in all regions of the country. The combined broadcasts on Sunday broadcast and Monday Night Playhouse, reaches up to 125,000 listeners.

Three plays from English language playwrights dealing with the topic of Immigration will be commissioned by Sunday Showcase. They will be produced in English and also translated and produced in French, and broadcast on the French language network. (Two plays originating in French are also being commissioned, produced and translated into English.)

The topic of Immigration can be interpreted broadly, both in terms of format and content, but playwrights should remember that Sunday Showcase broadcasts are 52 minutes in length. We are looking for original work written specifically for the medium of radio. The ideal proposal is two or three pages and should include a fairly detailed story outline and an indication from the playwright as to why this particular story needs to be told.